MATERNITY MAGIC

Empower and Discover Yourself while Planning for and Returning from Maternity Leave

ANNA MINTO

This book is dedicated to:

My parents, who taught me how to parent
(and continue to teach me)

My children, who journeyed along with me
(and survived the trip)

My clients, who delight me every day
(and so vulnerably share their experiences)

My family and friends, who tirelessly helped me
edit, format, and correct
(hopefully most of the errors)

Contents

PART FOUR:

PART FIVE:

Why This Book Exists

Congratulations! As my children's paternal grandma (a very Zen, sage Japanese woman) once told me, *"The Universe is about to shift. Imperceptibly, but definitively so."* She couldn't have put it more succinctly. Though I wasn't quite sure at the time what she was talking about. But I learned the wisdom in this truth. The universe did indeed shift … and so did the complexity, chaos, and love in my life.

I had read many pregnancy books (as most of us probably did), with my favorite being *What to Expect When You're Expecting.* I had dozens of baby and parenting books (though decades on, I can't recall what they were). And I felt totally, absolutely prepared and informed to be pregnant and deliver a baby. I would even tell myself, "You got this, girl!"

Then Charlotte arrived five weeks early and I had no clue what to do with a baby. The delivery room video sums it up as I exclaim: *"It's a baby!"* (I'm not sure quite what I was expecting, but she was, indeed, a baby).

Fortunately for me, my mum, Fran, had flown over to London for the birth, and provided all the guidance I craved, while having the wisdom to leave me to my own devices to learn. My dad, Clive, also happened to have been an exceptionally involved father to my sister and me right from the start. (This was quite unusual in the '60s and '70s. Do you know that most dads "didn't do diapers" in those days?) So, he too had sage advice and was very hands-on. Also,

Charlotte's father was an exceptionally involved and engaged dad. (He even changed all the diapers in the hospital.)

The "what do I do with this wild, pink, screaming person that is tinier than any human I have ever held?" phase went by relatively quickly and smoothly. I quickly learned how to be a mum, and a really good one (in my humble opinion). In the scheme of things, that part (the baby part) was surprisingly relatively smooth sailing. (Except the part where I tried bathing her alone, and she slipped under and a bubble came out of her nose, and she screamed when I pulled her back up. But that's another story.) We will all make parenting mistakes somewhere along the way. Guarantee it. Many of them.

The wisdom and support of My Tribe was there for me, especially in those early days of parenting.

The other piece of me—the driven-to-succeed, Type A, Myers-Briggs ENTJ, Enneagram Type 3 Achiever, Harvard MBA, skipped three grades, fast-track consultant at Boston Consulting Group—was completely in the dark. There were no books about "how to think about returning to work." (Even today, I've not come across any that I really like.) I oscillated from *"I'm never, ever going back to work"* to *"I need to work to be truly fulfilled, which will let me be the best mom."* It was trial by experimentation and speculation.

Over the next five years and one day, I welcomed Matthew and Sarah into the world. All three experiences were completely different. Charlotte was the "perfect" baby, had all the cuteness to go with it and an adoring "first" (child, grandchild, niece, etc.) following. Matthew was the first "boy" in our maternal lineage. He introduced himself as a toddler as "Matmew-No" and he might have been an only child if born first. Sarah was the fiercely independent one, whom we lost and couldn't find on several occasions. Interesting how totally unique and absolutely amazing they all are!

From a career perspective, I did part time (various combinations of 25, 50, 60, 80, and 100 percent). I took a three-month leave, a five-month leave, and a seven-month leave for different maternities. I stayed with Boston Consulting Group for 17 years, across four offices, leaving as a Managing Director and Partner and a Lead Officer of the global Consumer Practice and Organization Practice. I balanced the world of fast-paced consulting with parenting, family, friends, and community—though looking back on it, with little time for me. It worked, but I wish I'd had more guidance about returning to work, exploring my options, and deciding what was best for me and my family.

Fast-forward to more recent times. I founded a company called You Are Possible. Our mission is to *"Empower Women Executive Leaders to Thrive in Fast-Paced Environments."* A focus of the business is one-on-one coaching and executive advisory. From this, a specialty support topic emerged that we dubbed "Maternity Magic" (and later, "Parental Pivot" to include partners, but that's a whole other topic!). Maternity Magic Coaching Advisory supports amazing women journeying this critical life transition into parenting while still wanting to thrive in their careers and lives.

Over the years, I have observed the often-common challenges of these incredible women and shared with them what I've learned about how to think about the journey, what to capture from others, how to explore options, and how to have the courage to choose what feels right for them.

This book is for women executive leaders who are coming up on (or finishing up) a maternity leave, who want to explore not whether to return to her career, but rather how to best think about and prepare herself to thrive upon returning work with a baby in tow.

While the book may be small, it is mighty. It is not a "quick read," but rather an opportunity to sit back, reflect, and metabolize. Many chapters have space for you to jot down your thoughts and decisions. Other chapters point you to online resources and assessments. It is more of an interactive exploration and workbook than a "how to" book. Take the time to explore with pen and highlighter to hand.

May you discover what works best for you!

Anna

PART ONE

KNOW THYSELF

1. Three Foundational Concepts

2. What YOU Really Want

3. Where You Come From

4. Your Life Stage

5. Your Natural State

6. Mindset Matters

7. Mindfulness & Somatic Wisdom

8. Choosing Narratives

9. Taking Stock

10. You Can't Control the World

You may notice that this part of the book—"Know Thyself"—makes up over half of the content. There's a reason for this. Before getting into the specifics of "Maternity Magic" and planning for your upcoming leave, and then your return to work, you can benefit greatly from reviewing where you have come from, and where you aspire to go.

Of course, if you are already a fully developed, perpetually happy, mindful individual with incredible intuition and emotional intelligence, you can skip this section. If you're not quite there yet, take a peek in preparation for the journey into taking a leave and returning to work.

The following chapters suggest concepts and exercises to guide and inspire you. I encourage you to take liberal notes, jot things down, revisit and revise, and use the blank pages to fill in your story.

Have fun, and don't take yourself too seriously—it's a journey of discovery!

 PLEASE NOTE! 

Part One, *Know Thyself*, covers critical foundational topics
that are broadly applicable well beyond
the more narrowly defined subject of maternity leave.

Without deeply understanding yourself,
it is difficult to develop your negotiating strategy
to plan for and return from maternity leave.

Therefore, I have allocated half of this book
to exploring these topics of self-discovery.

If, however, you would prefer to jump straight into
specific maternity leave topics,
please proceed directly to Part 2 of this book, on page 123.

Three Foundational Concepts

Before we begin our journey through Maternity Magic, I'd like to introduce three quick concepts for you to consider as a foundation for your exploration and investment in yourself (like reading this book!).

In this chapter we'll explore:

    A. Protecting the Rocks

    B. Being Selfish

    C. Grounding

A. PROTECTING THE ROCKS

Priorities, priorities, priorities! Often a twin to the dreaded to-do list. I know very few people with the luxury of having "all the time in the world" all the time. So that means we make choices about what we do and how we spend our time.

There's an interesting experiment to try if you haven't seen it demonstrated before. Take a mason jar or other container. Find some rocks, pebbles, and sand. Try putting these items into the jar in two different ways:

Method 1: Pour the sand in the jar (say, halfway). Place enough pebbles on top of it to get to the rim of the jar. Now put the stones on top. Now try to put the lid on. It doesn't fit … at least it *shouldn't* fit because the stones are on top!

Method 2: Take everything out of the jar and put the same rocks in, but first. Then place the pebbles in. Now sprinkle in the sand. Put on the lid. Ta-da! It fits!

OK, so what's the moral of the story here? Imagine that the rocks represent the most important priorities in your life—the things that really matter to you, are life- and mission-critical. Pebbles represent the things that are lower priorities but nonetheless still important and/or urgent. Sand represents all those annoying little things that get in the way but don't add much value or happiness, yet "have" to be done. The lesson is that if we let all the smaller things in life fill our time and energy first, we will have no focus left for the things that are critical to our ambitions and well-being.

Photo credit: Deniz Altindas, Unsplash.com

Your Rocks:

____

____

____

____

Your Pebbles:

____

____

____

____

Your Sand:

____

____

____

____

B. BEING SELFISH

For most of us, the journey into motherhood is eye-opening, awe-inspiring, incredible, and exciting. On the flipside, it's also new, unknown, mysterious, mistake-laden, unpredictable, scary, exhausting, and often filled with fear of failure, uncertainty, and anxiety. It can be overwhelming. And that's just the "parenting" side of the equation. Then there's the rest of life ("when life gets lifey," as a friend of mine says)—and not to mention work.

It's easy to get lost in work pre-baby, and then in new mommy-ness post-baby. To take care of the baby, the family, the partner, the friends, the community, and all those other people. Somehow, we forget to take care of the most important person—ourselves. If we are not happy, and growing, and living, and thriving … well, to put it politely, we tend to not put our best selves forward. In the extreme, we become people who are not nice to be around. We don't prioritize our self-care, and we are not being self-ish enough.

"Selfish" gets a bad rap these days, implying (incorrectly) "at the expense of others." If there's a finite number of coconuts on a deserted island and I take one extra, someone else gets one less. In some ways, we live in a world of finite. Finite energy, time, water, and food, for example.

I propose that self-care and "selfishness" live in the world of the infinite, not the world of the finite. Things like love, creativity, and passion live in the infinite world. Taking time to boost ourselves up does not rob time from others and make them go down.

Self-care is not selfish. It's self-ish. Being self-ish is a good thing. A really good thing. It's about caring about "me." Which is also good for "them." It lifts us up and helps us be better leaders in our personal and professional lives—and that makes the world a better place for those around us.

Self: *(as noun) A person's essential being that distinguishes them from others, especially considered as the object of introspection or reflexive action.*

Ish: (yes, it's in the dictionary): *(adverb): To some extent.*

Have you considered scheduling an exquisite weekly self-care "hour of indulgence" with your self-ish self? To do the things that bring you joy. To take that luxurious bubble bath. To sing in the shower. To dance in the rain. To dig your hands in the garden. To just sit and be. To do whatever it is that does it for you—the things you love that bring you joy. Indulge your self-ish self. For your sake and for the sake of those around you.

Even indulge in reading this book in a quiet spot, giving yourself space to learn and explore. The investment in you is worth it.

Bubble bath, anyone?

Source: Shutterstock.com

C. GROUNDING

Back in the days of the caveman and our life on the savanna, we evolved to be highly aware of our surroundings and monitor for danger. When presented with a threat, we shifted to high alert and released stress hormones to accelerate our impending fight-or-flight reactions. The brainstem is wired to do this unconsciously, even today.

Well, we don't live in caves anymore (at least most of us don't, the wi-fi would suck and electricity would be hard to wire up), yet we still possess this instinct. While lions may not roam our streets, we are still wired for reaction to inputs. In today's busy world, there are way more "alert inputs" than we humans used to have when we were quietly picking berries in peaceful meadows.

We are bombarded with "stressors" today. Incessantly. As a result, our minds tell our bodies to tense up and get prepared for action. And our tensed-up, fragmented, reactive bodies let our minds know that so that we can be prepared for danger. Then our minds tell our bodies to tense up further. The infinite cycle reinforces itself.

Without even being aware of it, our tensed-up bodies, in a state of high alert, are keeping us on edge and distract us from being fully present in the now. There's a whole bunch of literature on what stress hormones do to our health and longevity (and I'll leave it for others to explain). I'll just say it's not pretty.

If you don't believe me about the stressed mind-body connection, try this one-minute exercise. (I really do mean try it!)

Take a slow (slow!), luxurious neck roll in one direction, and then in the other. Notice anything? Almost everyone reports stiffness or soreness, and sometimes even crackling or popping sounds. That's stress-tension release.

To break the mind-body stress cycle and be fully present in the moment, there is a simple two-minute technique you can do to release pressure and become more fully present. It's called "Grounding." Here's how it works:

- Sit up comfortably on your chair (or stand, if you prefer), arms relaxed with hands on your lap (or at your sides) and unclenched.

- Close your eyes (well, after reading all the directions here!).

- Take five slow, deep cleansing breaths, counting each one. Pause.

- Then scan and release tension in your body, starting at the very top of your head and working all the way down your body, naming the parts. Scalp, temples, cheeks, mouth, tongue, jaw, neck, collarbone. Keep going down to the tips of your toes.

- When you reach your toes, take one more deep breath, and when you are ready, gently open your eyes, returning to your present space.

- *Aaaahhhhh.* Feel better?

Notice how different you feel, and the impact it has on calming and focusing your mind on the issue(s) at hand. This can be done any time. It only takes two minutes. Some people start and/or end their days with it; others find it useful before meetings or when switching activities. Whatever works for you.

Can you commit to trying it out a couple of times a day, say, for the next week? Nothing to lose if it doesn't do much for you, other than 14 minutes of your life.

Now that you've grasped these three foundational concepts (Protecting Rocks, Being Selfish, and Grounding), let's continue on the journey of Knowing Yourself.

What YOU Really Want

In this chapter we'll explore four key ideas:

    A. (Revisiting) Your Purpose

    B. Vision Boards

    C. Values

    D. Ikigai

No human being is the same as another human being, just like no two snowflakes are identical. Some people are more like others, and some people are less like others. I think of it like a garden. Each plant is unique and special in its own beautiful way. But each one seeks different sources of energy, nutrients in the soil, levels of moisture, and amounts of sunshine. Like plants in a garden, each of us humans has different needs in order to best thrive.

This chapter will guide you through discovering your unique you. Because until you fully understand yourself (as much as one ever can), it's unrealistic to develop a plan that best suits your needs and aspirations.

Each of the suggested explorations that follow is designed to be a thoughtful, ongoing, iterative process. It's not "one and done," but rather a creative, playful enquiry. There are no right answers. It is worth investing the time and thought, especially before your priority "rocks" expand to encompass your impending arrival—which is a huge rock!

Photo credit: Jade Seok, Unsplash.com

A. (REVISITING) YOUR PURPOSE

Everyone has a "Purpose" in life. Few of us actually ever articulate it. While almost every company, organization and group define theirs, we rarely define ours. If we are the "CEO of Me," then we should probably be clear on what "me" is here to do.

A Personal Purpose Statement is a simple sentence that captures the essence of what one believes they are here on earth to do and to be. For example, my (ever emerging) Purpose is:

"I empower people to thrive in the kaleidoscope of life"

Other examples from my clients include:

- "I create bold communities by connecting the dots"

- "I make the world a safer place"

- "I shine a light so others can see"

- "I support the communities I live in to be more harmonious"

You get the drift. So, what's your Purpose? What's your magical power?

Here's some space for you to iterate and explore.

"My Purpose in Life is to ..."

____

____

____

____

____

It looks super simple once completed, yet it takes a lot of soaking time and reflection to really crisp up your Purpose.

If you're having difficulty, start by picking a sentence that roughly describes yourself and iterate on that idea as the days go by. The shorter, simpler, and more visual you can be, the better. It's hard to remember a whole paragraph about your Purpose. A single sentence can distill it to something memorable.

B. VISION BOARDS

Knowing your Purpose in life is the critical starting point, but what does it mean? How does it look? What does it feel like? That's where Vision Boards come in. They translate the "why" (Purpose) to the "what" (Vision). They look forward to the next 1–5 years, to show the kinds of things you "do" that bring your Purpose to life.

They make it real. And they will evolve over time. (Some clients revisit their Vision Boards every year, as circumstances shift, and new experiences and opportunities emerge.)

Here's how to create one for yourself:

- Set aside 15 minutes in your calendar outside of work hours. Sit in a quiet, uninterrupted place. Maybe even light a scented candle with music you enjoy and grab a snack to nibble on.

- Begin by Grounding (which we covered earlier).

- Take a fresh, crisp blank piece of paper, and some colored pens and pencils. Draw symbols and words and ideas about what matters most to you. Doodle. Get creative, use sparkles. Google images or quotes. Cut and paste, like you did in kindergarten! Whatever sings from your heart and soul. There's no right or wrong answer!

- Draw upon reflections made in your journal if you keep one.

- Start with a first pass, then at a set (calendared) time each week, revisit it and either add to it, edit it, or completely restart it. Each time, expand and refine what that looks and feels like. Make it yours, and in your style.

Here are some examples of how different and unique they can be:

C. VALUES

Values aren't chosen. They evolve and emerge with life experiences, wisdom, and time. They are a central part of our core being. They highlight what we stand for—our personal code of conduct. Identifying those values explicitly can make our lives more consistent and fulfilling. If we don't, our behaviors can be inconsistent and lack cohesion. That makes us grumpy—and others around us grumpy.

Here's an approach to identifying your own personal core values, adapted from Scott Jeffrey's "7 Steps to Discovering Your Core Values," www.ScottJeffrey.com.

1. *Ground yourself* (see Chapter 1) and put yourself in a space of open-mindedness—a mindset where we are unlocked for learning. Create a place for quiet reflection and contemplation and grab a pen and some paper.

2. *Glance over some ideas* of what personal core values can be. There are plenty of lists of core values online. Some of them have as many as several hundred listed. Following are a little over 200 suggestions you might consider to get your brain warmed up. But don't limit yourself to that list as we proceed. Just use it as potential thought starters.

3. *Start writing your list.* Just write what comes to mind. If you get stuck (and yes, most of us do!) try these three approaches that can help unveil your values:

   a. *Best experiences.* Think of a meaningful experience that stands out for you in a positive way. Ask yourself: *What was going on? What made it so special? What values were you honoring at that time?*

CATEGORIES OF CORE VALUES...A STARTER LIST OF IDEAS

ACHIEVEMENT
Accomplishment
Ambition
Capable
Challenge
Competence
Credibility
Determination
Development
Drive
Effectiveness
Empower
Endurance
Excellence
Famous
Greatness
Growth
Hard work
Improvement
Influence
Intensity
Leadership
Mastery
Motivation
Performance
Persistence
Potential
Power
Productivity
Professionalism
Prosperity
Recognition
Results-oriented
Risk
Significance
Skill
Skillfulness
Status
Success
Talent
Victory
Wealth
Winning

COURAGE
Bravery
Conviction
Fearless
Valor

CREATIVITY
Creation
Curiosity
Discovery
Exploration
Expressive
Imagination
Innovation
Inquisitive
Intuitive
Openness
Originality
Uniqueness
Wonder

ENJOYMENT
Amusement
Enthusiasm
Experience
Fun
Playfulness
Recreation
Spontaneous
Surprise

FREEDOM
Independence
Individuality
Liberty

HEALTH
Body image
Calm
Energy
Fitness
Strength
Vitality

INTEGRITY
Accountability
Candor
Commitment
Dependability
Dignity
Honesty
Honor
Responsibility
Sincerity
Transparency
Trust

Trustworthy
Truth

INTELLIGENCE
Brilliance
Clever
Common sense
Decisiveness
Foresight
Genius
Insightful
Knowledge
Learning
Logic
Openness
Realistic
Reason
Reflective
Smart
Thoughtful
Understanding
Vision
Wisdom

FEELINGS
Acceptance
Comfort
Compassion
Contentment
Empathy
Grace
Gratitude
Happiness
Hope
Inspiring
Irreverent
Joy
Kindness
Love
Optimism
Passion
Peace
Poise
Respect
Reverence
Satisfaction
Serenity
Thankful
Tranquility
Welcoming

ORDER
Accuracy
Careful
Certainty
Cleanliness
Consistency
Control
Decisive
Economy
Justice
Lawful
Moderation
Organization
Security
Stability
Structure
Thorough
Timeliness

PRESENCE
Alertness
Attentive
Awareness
Beauty
Calm
Clear
Concentration
Focus
Silence
Simplicity
Solitude

SPIRITUALITY
Adaptability
Altruism
Balance
Charity
Communication
Community
Connection
Consciousness
Contribution
Cooperation
Courtesy
Devotion
Equality
Ethical
Fairness
Family
Fidelity

Friendship
Generosity
Giving
Goodness
Harmony
Humility
Loyalty
Maturity
Meaning
Selfless
Sensitivity
Service
Sharing
Spirit
Stewardship
Support
Sustainability
Teamwork
Tolerance
Unity

STRENGTH
Assertiveness
Boldness
Confidence
Dedication
Discipline
Ferocious
Fortitude
Persistence
Power
Restraint
Rigor
Self-reliance
Temperance
Toughness
Vigor
Will

b. *Worst experiences.* Go to the opposite extreme and think of an experience that made you mad, frustrated, or sad. Ask yourself: *What was going on? What were you feeling? What values were you suppressing at that time?*

c. *Code of conduct.* Think about what is most important for you to have in your life (beyond meeting basic needs and surviving). Ask yourself: *What must you have to be fulfilled? What gives you energy and pleasure?*

4. *Group like things together.* Look for common themes, such as the categories in the example value lists above (achievement, courage, creativity, etc.). Within each group, highlight the most important by circling them. Minimize the less important by bracketing them. You should now have a messy piece of paper with lots of notes, scratch-outs and chaos.

5. Prioritize and zoom in. From the messy paper in step 4, consider taking a fresh piece of paper and prioritizing those that really (really) resonate with you. Too few, and you won't really capture the integral you. Too many, and you won't be likely to remember them all. Most clients settle in on a half dozen to a dozen or so.

6. Expand. Not the list of values, but the description or color behind them. It's hard to remember a generic laundry list of values and adding descriptors or emotional context can help clarify. For example, "I value honesty because it lets me have a clear conscience, which helps me feel free to be me."

7. Revise. Not immediately. Give yourself a break. Come back to your list of core values every couple of days for as often as you like, refining the list to ensure that they:

- Inspire you
- Reflect the true you
- Trigger an emotional feeling
- Are consistent
- Play to your strengths
- Are meaningful and memorable
- Are prioritized

8. Rate yourself. Give yourself a score on a scale of 1–10 for each and notice where you are today in living your personal core values. Where you rate yourself low, decide what you are going to do to change that. Where they are high, keep doing what you are doing.

As you move forward into planning and returning from your leave, these crystal-clear thoughts about values will guide clarity in the decisions you will be making. Keep it close at hand!

D. IKIGAI

生き甲斐

(OK, I am trusting that the Japanese symbols above do indeed translate to the word "Ikigai"!)

Ikigai is a Japanese concept about being. There isn't a good translation of the word into English or Western languages. It describes the balance between:

- What you love and are good at (passions and talents); and

- What the world (or organization) needs and is willing to pay for

Once a week, sit in a quiet place for 15 minutes. Put it on your calendar (or it is unlikely to happen) and commit to it. (It's only 15 minutes, after all.) Grab paper and pen(s), and make yourself comfortable in a special, quiet place. Perhaps this space includes soft music, a candle, a calming aromatherapy scent. Do what pleases you. Shut the door and ask not to be interrupted. (Almost *anything* can wait 15 minutes, can't it? OK, well maybe not a fire, but that's pretty unlikely to happen.)

Begin by taking a deep cleansing breath and Grounding yourself. (Remember your one-minute body-scan exercise described in the first chapter?). Then sit quietly and:

- Contemplate the application of this in your life today.

- Think about how the framework pertains to your upcoming new role or life-phase.

Jot down your thoughts here over the next couple of weeks. Draw. Use images and sparkly pens. Get creative. Have fun. Iterate. Think deep. Here's some space for you:

Where You Come From

This chapter is quite different from the last, which was present and forward-looking in considering your Purpose, Vision, and Ikigai. Here, we will explore the past—your origins, roots, and journey—as clues that delve deep into the essence of who you are today.

In this chapter we'll explore:

A. Childhood Essence—"I Am..."

B. Essential Positive Quality

C. Kintsugi

A. CHILDHOOD ESSENCE—"*I AM ...*"

Begin by finding a photo of yourself when you were younger (ahem, much younger). Something that captures that innocence, playfulness, and happiness of you as a child. Here's the photo I use for myself:

Photo credit: my parents

Start by Grounding yourself and becoming fully present. Find a quiet spot, with soft light, a comfy seat, and no interruptions. Make sure you have paper and pen(s). This exercise will take about 15 minutes.

Look deeply into the eyes of that child. Look into her essence and soul. Complete the sentence "*I am …*" multiple times and jot down the words that come to mind. Look for the positive.

Avoid the temptation to become too analytical or rational and just let your thoughts flow. Avoid surfacing any negative thoughts or resentments. This is all about the magical powers of your younger self. Take 5–10 minutes to explore deeply.

Now go look at yourself in the mirror. Stare deep into your eyes. What do you see? Is that essence still there? Let me be clear here, we're not looking in the mirror to critique ourselves, comment on our wrinkly happy-lines eyes, or note the spinach in our teeth. Take five minutes to celebrate the power and essence of you. Just you. See how the current now still has the essence of the you then, though sometimes it is hidden well beneath our seasoned exterior.

I realize that this exercise seems odd on paper (and that you might think I'm a bit woo-woo crazy) but please just try it. My clients tell me it's an enlightening experience. I found it so revealing that I now keep a copy of that photo on my desk to remind me of who "*I am …*"

B. ESSENTIAL POSITIVE QUALITY

An essential positive quality (or EPQ) is a term that describes a core virtue or essence you embody, which has remained with you throughout life, like a golden thread weaving your path. It's a quality that embodies the deepest you, and a value or virtue that you hold deeply. Sure, there are lots of nice things you can say about yourself.

But the EPQ gets to the heart of the matter and shines through us always (well, almost always).

Stop and think about yours for a moment. What might it be? What's the short list? What would your friends and family say? What did you already discover about your values in Chapter 2?

Here's a (not exhaustive) list of some EPQs you might highlight or consider. Circle those that MOST represent you, then keep narrowing it down. What's the short list? Perhaps your words aren't even on the list! What's the word or two that is you?

ESSENTIAL POSITIVE QUALITIES...A STARTER LIST

Analytical	Devotion	Honesty	Passionate	Stability
Appreciative	Dignity	Humility	Patience	Steadfastness
Balanced	Driven	Innocence	Perseverance	Strength
Calm	Enduring	Insightful	Persistence	Soft
Caring	Energy	Integrity	Playful	Tenacity
Champion	Enthusiasm	Intentional	Power	Tender
Clarity	Faith	Joyful	Preparedness	Transparency
Compassion	Fierce	Justice	Protective	Trustworthy
Courageous	Flexible	Kindness	Purity	Understanding
Creativity	Generosity	Love	Purposeful	Warmth
Curiosity	Generous heart	Loyalty	Regal	Welcoming
Decisive	Graciousness	Majesty	Resilience	Wisdom
Deep	Gratitude	Mysterious	Responsible	Wonder
Defender	Grounded	Nobility	Self-awareness	
Determined	Helpfulness	Openness	Selflessness	

Now that you (hopefully) have one or a couple in mind, reflect on it. Where has it shone through? Where has it carried you through? How has it evolved? Why is it such a part of you?

Hold it tight! It reflects the essence of "you"!

My EPQ:

C. KINTSUGI

金継ぎ

(Yet again, I do hope that these symbols translate to what I am told they are, or someone is having a great joke on me.)

Photo credit: Motoki Tonn, Unsplash.com

Kintsugi, which means "golden joinery," is the Japanese art of putting broken pottery pieces back together with lacquer-dusted powdered gold, silver, or platinum. Weaving together parts with a golden seam to create the beautiful whole.

As we explore our desires moving forward and what we "want," it can be helpful to look backward and reflect on where we've been and how it's shaping our lives today.

As we journey through life, we've all experienced breakages and parts of us that were difficult to experience, or things that we wish we had done differently. The past is the past and we can't change it; and the future is the future and is not controllable or known. But in the present, we can reflect on those fragmented pieces, and how they can be put together to reflect the wholeness of your beautiful you. After all, we wouldn't be where we are today if we hadn't journeyed through our past experiences.

To reflect on this, set aside 30 minutes in a quiet spot, maybe even with scented candles and soft music, and pull out a reflection journal. (Note the "journal" theme here. If you don't keep or have one, consider picking one out and keeping it, though of course keep it well hidden from prying eyes.

Ask yourself: "*What were the toughest parts of my life?*" Write down a handful, or even a dozen. Include even those experiences you would rather not have happened. Pause. Take some deep breaths.

Then ask yourself, "*How did it contribute to who I am today?*" and "*What did I learn from it?*" and "*What 'gifts' are hidden in the bad ?*" Jot your thoughts down. Then reflect on all your collective thoughts.

Consider where you might have gratitude for some elements of those experiences. There's almost always a gift or a lesson hidden in the bad. It's interesting to see how all our past creates who we are today, and who we might become in our future.

Notes to self:

____

____

____

____

____

____

Your Life Stage

In this chapter we'll explore four concepts:

    A. Lifetime Line

    B. Jet Ski, Canoe, Catamaran

    C. Adult Development "Ways of Being"

    D. Six Streams of Competence

A. LIFETIME LINE

Our human lives are actually quite short.

Here is a 90-year lifespan in years, with each row representing a decade:

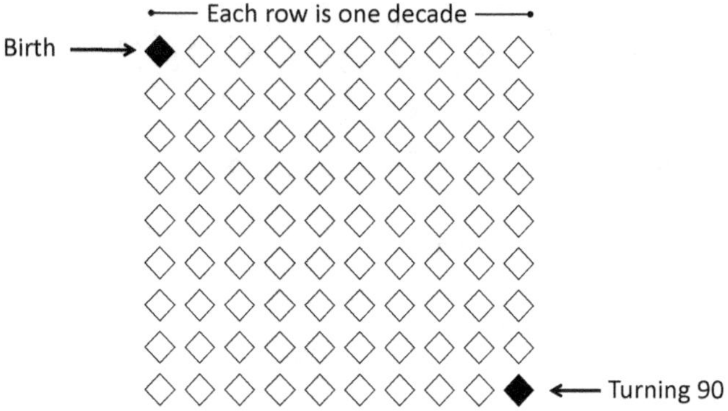

And here it is in months, with each row representing three years for a total of 1,080 months:

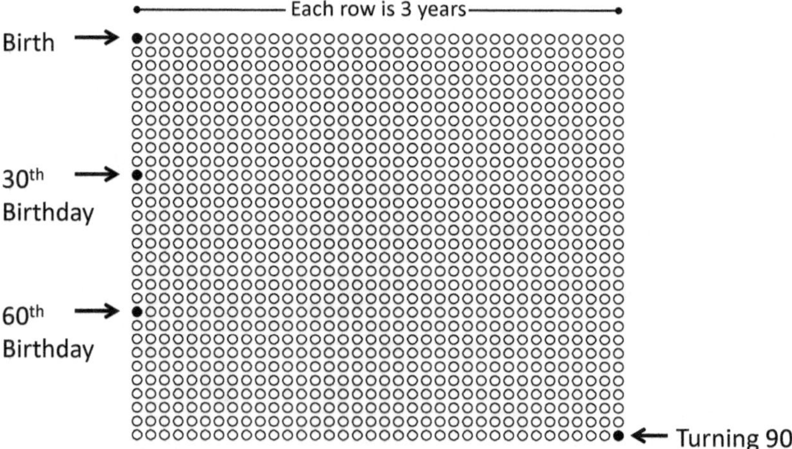

And finally in weeks, with each row representing a year for a total of 4,680 weeks:

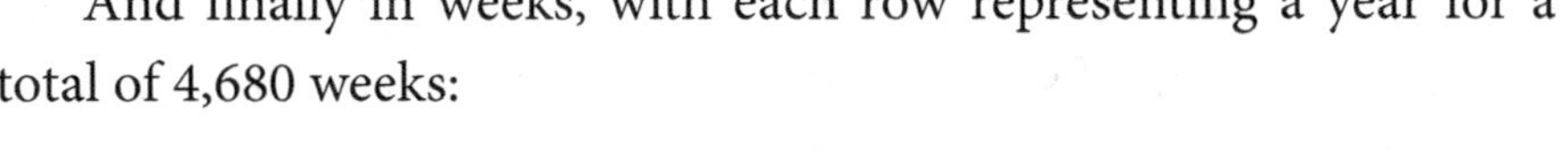

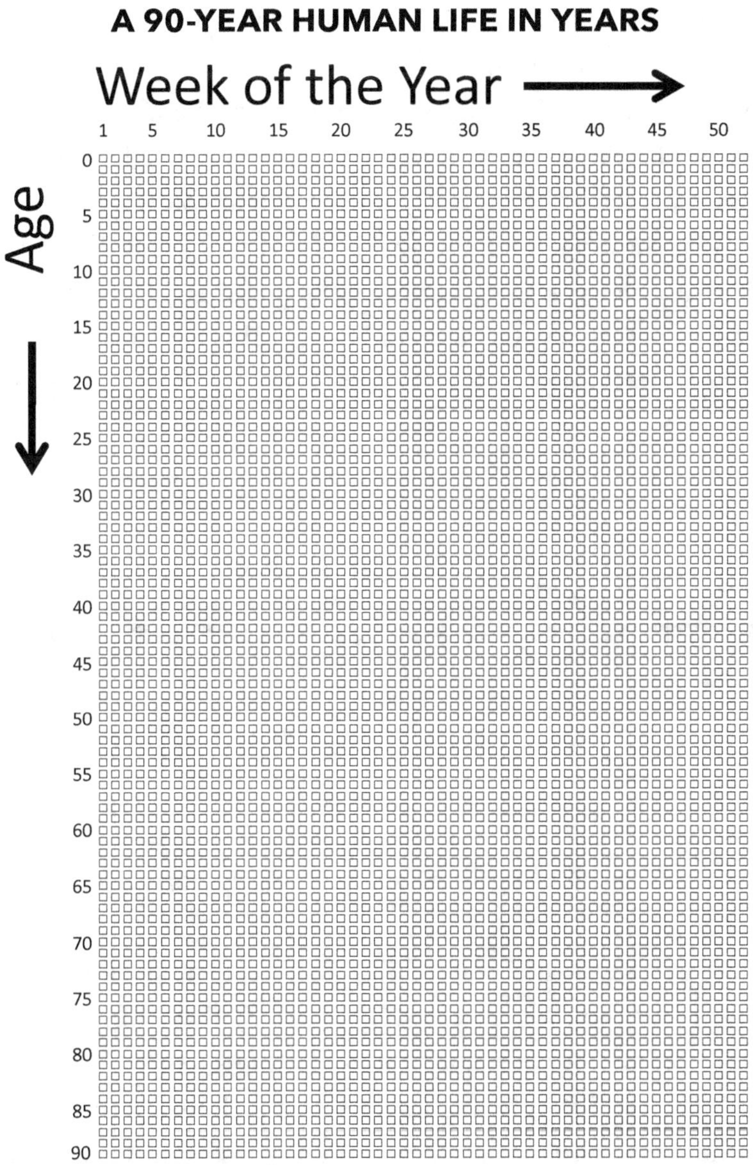

Maybe it's just me, but it doesn't sound like a lot of time. Some weeks seem to just fly by, especially as we get older. On the other hand, that's a lot of dots, and you're not even halfway through them (unless, of course, you get hit by a bus tomorrow, but that may be even less likely than winning the lottery).

So, let's pull it all back to the perspective of "you."

Take a piece of paper and put a "0" on the left side of the page. The zero represents the start of your life, when you were born. Now make a guess at how long you will live and write that down on the right side of the page. (Yes, I know we're getting a bit morbid here.) Draw a line between your birth and death. This is your life timeline. Mark your current age with a big star.

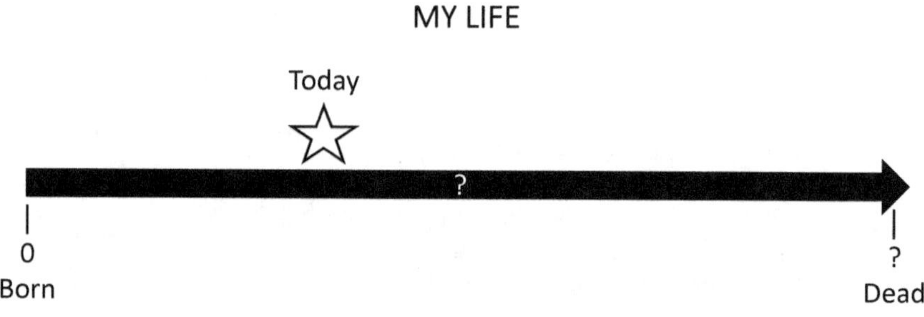

Now let's divide that line up into a half dozen or so "life segments," drawing dividing lines at the roughly correct spot on the timeline.

The early segments (say, childhood, teen, and college years) are what I call the *should* years. There are a lot of things we really "should" do: learning to tie our shoes, getting a degree if we wish to go into business. After the early *should* years, there are the *my choice* years where we choose what to do and how we want to do it. Notable events might include marriage(s), child(ren), retirement (active), and retirement (fully nursing home supported).

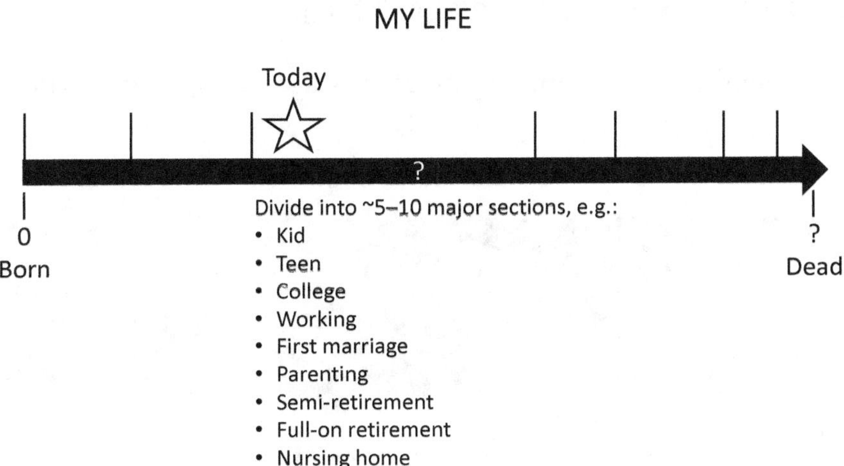

Sitting and reflecting on their life on one page, my clients are often surprised by what they see. In particular, they note how long the "working" stage often is, and how relatively early on they start their lifetime career. The point here is to think about where you are in life—where you've been and where you might go. This exercise puts in perspective your about-to-be-parent milestone, and its career implications.

Here's a space for you to noodle on:

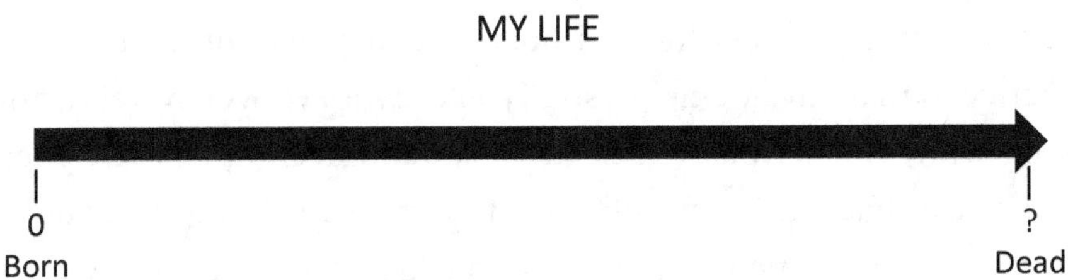

B. JET SKI, CANOE, CATAMARAN

Here's another way of thinking about life stages, using a boat analogy.

THE LIFE STAGE YOU ARE IN

Sources: Unsplash.com.
Photo credits: Sea Doo – Alice Challies, Canoe – Getty Images, Catamaran – Miquel Gelabert

The *Jet Ski®* is a rapid exploration vehicle for our earliest years, when we are largely just worried about ourselves. We zoom around, exploring the world and having fun. And we can pretty much do what we want when we want, independently (and sometimes, depending on our personalities, recklessly). We're focused on ourselves, though occasionally we'll pick up (and drop off) a passenger or two and take them along for the ride.

The *canoe* represents the middle stage of life, often in partnership with others. The open water can narrow to a fast-moving stream, carrying you along with twists, turns, and dangers. You often paddle the rapids with another on board, requiring coordination and practice to maneuver. One person (you or whoever you're venturing along with) can seriously rock the boat, and even tip it over. Their actions can have a significant impact on your realities. The couple's survival is interdependent (unless you kick them out to swim to shore, but yet again, that's a topic for another book). It's exhilarating and unpredictable. Adding in a baby as passenger only increases the complexity and caution. The adventure is largely into the unknown.

And it's fast-paced, unpredictable, and constantly changing. Agility becomes critical.

The *catamaran* represents a slower, more stable later phase of life. Perhaps one in which we've empty-nested, and maybe even retired. (That seems far off, but it will indeed happen one day.) The boat is stable and there's more smooth sailing.

One person's actions are not likely to sink the ship, and you have more flexibility to do things independently, though you can chart courses together. It's a more stable, predictable, calm stage of life.

So, let's face it: Since you're reading this book, you are probably pregnant and expecting a baby soon. This means you are firmly in a canoe and approaching some turbulence in upcoming Class 6 extreme rapids. Hold on tight and start paddling! Recognize, acknowledge, and accept the stage of life you are in.

C. ADULT DEVELOPMENT "WAYS OF BEING"

I bet you've already picked up books on infant, baby, and toddler development. These will be followed by a multitude of books on raising teenagers and adolescents. (Good luck with that. You'll need strength and patience, but they do come out the other side, and miraculously you will regain your status as an intelligent person—again, a topic for another book.)

But have you ever read a book about the states of *adult* development? I sure hadn't until I got into coaching and executive advisory. And I wish I had, because it's so blatantly obvious (and reassuring to know that your path is "normal"). It's amazing to me that leaders, who tend to rely heavily on information and analysis, were not given this information way earlier in life. It should be a core high school curriculum course!

If you haven't heard about this, read on. There are apparently 10 levels of adult developmental "Ways of Being." But I'll focus on the first five because a nearly infinitesimal number of people are scattered over the remaining five upper levels. I'm envisioning that those people are primarily monks living in a monastery, enlightening and growing themselves to higher levels of consciousness. In case you are interested, those upper levels are: *6. Freedom from Assessment, 7. Freedom from Meaninglessness, 8. Freedom from Narcissism, 9. Freedom from Suffering,* and *10. Freedom from Death.* I don't know about you, but I'm nowhere near those upper levels, at least for now and probably forever.

So, back to us mortal humans…

The 10 developmental "Ways of Being" describe an adult development journey. I am going to paraphrase and adapt liberally here from the writings of James Flaherty, in his book *Integral Coaching.* (The book has some deep and interesting thinking in it, if you're so inclined.)

Here are highlights and caveats about our adult development:

- Development moves in one direction only, and unfolds in a particular natural order.

- It's not inevitable; it requires our active participation.

- Most of us don't listen until there's a (midlife) crisis.

- The levels build on each other, and no one is permanently at one level.

- We can be at different levels for different dimensions within our lives.

- Higher ("deeper") does not mean better.

- We can only be in the life that we have at this moment.

Now what are these first five levels?

1. Addressing Immediate Concerns

2. Balance

3. Conversations

4. Power

5. Vocation

Here's a description of each of the levels:

1. **Addressing Immediate Concerns**
   The most constrained level, when the world seems to be on fire. No learning, no preparation, no reserves. We're doing our best to keep our heads above water, save the people we care about, and get to safety. This is survival mode.

2. **Balance**
   We're just so busy, we don't have time to do anything. Every moment is jammed with multiple tasks; booked and over-booked. It's hard to separate our likes from what is healthy. We are loath to give up anything. We believe we are indispensable. High activity is disguised as a sense of meaning. We may brag about the number of hours we work, often with a gnawing fear that we're not so important. We're keeping all the juggling balls in the air.

3. **Conversations**
   We're becoming more proficient in speaking and listening, and we're able to see other people's views as just as valid as our own. We're willing to refrain from attacking others with different views, but still do not see them as equal. We have

discovered asking for what we want and negotiating what is requested of us. We are open and curious about what others know, and have the capacity to speak and listen from multiple perspectives without being unduly attached to any one of them. We learn to listen, and we catch on that the world is not just based on facts.

4. **Power**

Power in this context means having what we intend to happen in the world actually happen in a way that unifies us and contributes to others. It means attending to the kind of person we are becoming and living in the world that consequently opens. It is not about force, but it can turn into it. The human world is eternally fluid, shaped by how we speak in it and how we listen to it. We become present, focused, patient, resilient, creative, and steady in our personal sense of worth. We've overcome procrastination, settling, and justifying. We look courageously and dispassionately at ourself and our life, asking, "*How do I do this?*" rather than "*Can I do this?*" It is still about getting what we want for ourselves.

5. **Vocation**

This step up is a large one that most people never make. In this level, life is not about what I want, but rather about what life wants from me. It's about listening to the call of life, *Vocation*. Vocation is not a job, or a matter of willpower. Many people "visit" a stage of Vocation. It's a transformation because it's a complete reorientation of our world. We quiet ourselves so we can hear our inner call and wait to respond to whatever unfolds in front of us. Fear is much diminished, and we take on deeper trust of life as it unfolds. We find a place of profound meaning and belonging. Do not confuse this with fame, status, wealth, or even "making a difference." We are true to our intention and aligned with the best expressions of wisdom, compassion, integrity, and well-being. The essence of Vocation is surrender and the death of our self-importance and mechanisms of defense. So few reach this level because we're too attached to what we like, and we haven't found out how to trust. The evolution of our Vocation is not usually a dramatic one.

With that little educational detour about adult development wrapped up, what do you do with your newfound knowledge? I'd like to suggest that you pause and reflect on where you are, across different parts of your life. Where have you been, when? Where is your growth-edge?

One thing's for sure: The arrival of the baby can draw you to the "balance" stage like a magnet. Consider yourself forewarned!

WHERE I AM IN DEVELOPMENT

Immediate Needs	Balance	Conversations	Power	Vocation

D. SIX STREAMS OF COMPETENCE

Here's one last educational framework for thinking about where you are in your life. This section is adapted from materials shared in my Integral Coaching Certification with New Ventures West (an excellent school and community if you are considering becoming a coach).

This framework has "Streams of Competence" that independently and interdependently shape us. They are Cognitive, Emotional, Somatic, Relational, Spiritual, and Integrating. Unlike the "Ways of Being" we just reviewed, there is no order or hierarchy—they are simply different aspects (or pillars) of ourselves, and each can be at a different stage of development.

Cognitive

The ability to make observations in a particular field of activity and then to synthesize them into a coherent understanding. "Understanding" means seeing possibilities for action, making accurate predictions, and foreseeing potential breakdowns. *It's about taking a logical approach.*

Emotional

The ability to discern your own emotional states, what you are feeling at this moment, what is the background emotional tone of your life, what emotions are present when you experience difficulties, and other observations. Also, the ability to discern the emotional state of others, even when they themselves may be oblivious to it or denying it. This includes the ability to stay present and available to relationship and in communication amid strong emotional events (yours or others'). *It's about knowing the range of emotions and expanding the language.*

Somatic

The ability to observe what is happening in your body, e.g., feeling energized, tired, heavy, open, or tight. It's being able to tap into the wisdom of your body, which may have different insight into what's happening than your intellect or emotions. *This is not about whether you go to the gym 24/7, but rather about how you embody it.*

Relational

The ability to initiate and sustain mutually satisfying relationships. This includes being able to listen deeply and communicate profoundly with a wide variety of individuals and groups. It also includes the ability to compromise, see the world from different viewpoints, and be supportive of others' intentions; the ability to set aside one's own desires for the sake of the relationship while maintaining a sense of your own worth and dignity. *It's about being open to new networks of support and allowing multiple perspectives.*

Spiritual

The ability to create a life dedicated to the benefit of everyone, not only for the advantage of yourself, your family, company, or clan. This means the competence to initiate and sustain practices that strengthen your bond to the wide web of life connecting all people, all living systems, all things. This also includes developing yourself as an active member in communities dedicated to compassion, wisdom, and service to others. *It's about how we can trust the universe or web of life; it's NOT about organized religion, per se.*

Integrating

The ability to eliminate all the ways you compartmentalize your life so that your commitments, learning, and values are present in all your words, thoughts, actions, and relationships. It requires that you confront what you've been denying, avoiding, and justifying and that you be open to continuous learning and input from others. *It's about being the same person in all parts of life, integrating postures, values, and masculine & feminine sides.*

Again, having read this, sit back, and reflect on yourself. Where are you in each of the streams? Which are more or are less developed for you? Which might challenge you after the arrival of the baby and its dramatic shift in your universe?

6 STREAMS OF COMPETENCE

Cognitive	Emotional	Somatic

Relational	Spiritual	Integrating

Your Natural State

In this chapter we'll explore:

     A. Enneagram

     B. Clifton Strengths

     C. Myers-Briggs (MBTI)

     D. DiSC

There are a ton of "self-assessment" tools out there, with varying validity, explanations, and costs. It may seem odd to you that we are covering self-assessment in a book about maternity magic. But I truly believe pregnancy is a golden opportunity to stand back before the chaos of a new baby and reflect on where you have come from, where you are now, and how you aspire to grow.

My number one go-to tool is the Enneagram. (Without it, I would have difficulty understanding where my clients are growing from.) I also see good value in the MBTI (Myers-Briggs Type Indicator), DiSC, and Clifton Strengths, so I've included them here for your consideration. All are available online and are well validated. Some are more complex, others simpler; some more broadly deployed, others less so; some more deeply explored, others a one-shot opinion. There is a ton of literature and books out there on each if you are interested in deep diving. This will give you the bird's-eye overview.

What follows is a snapshot of my four favorites. Leverage them for what they're worth in your own diagnostic tool kit.

A. ENNEAGRAM

The Enneagram is, in the world of psychology, what Myers-Briggs (MBTI) seems to be in the world of business. Both are heavily validated and broadly used. In my opinion, the Enneagram has four key advantages over the MBTI, because:

- It focuses on behavioral "whys" (the roots behind an action) rather than the behaviors themselves.

- There are paths to growth and development.

- It highlights how behaviors migrate under conditions of stress and of security.

- It's simple—there are nine "Polarities," which are organized into triads ("Pearls") grounded in the gut, heart, or head.

The following table summarizes how it is organized.

ENNEAGRAM OVERVIEW

RED PEARLS	**GREEN PEARLS**	**BLUE PEARLS**
Gut, Instinct, Reality, Impact Present Anger	Heart, Feeling, Self, Seen Past Worth	Mind, Thinking, Separated, Security Future Fear
8: Challenger 9: Peacemaker 1: Reformer	2: Helper 3: Achiever 4: Individualist	5: Investigator 6: Thinker 7: Enthusiast

We all have some red, green, and blue in us. Some of us are more anchored in one or two than others.

The *red pearls* are driven from the gut. It's all about instinct and facing reality in the present. They look for how they are impacting the world and how the world impacts them. They operate on an "anger" continuum, which can be a mild grumbly "grrrr" in the belly, or in the extreme, rage and fieriness.

The *green pearls* are driven from the heart. It's all about feeling and being seen by others. Projecting their self-image is important. They spend much time thinking about the past. They operate on a "self-worth" continuum, which can be mildly expressed as feeling embarrassed or "less than," or in the extreme can be pride, vanity, or shame.

The *blue pearls* are driven by the thinking head. They separate and compartmentalize analytically. They want to feel safe and secure about the future. They operate on a "fear" continuum, which can be expressed in a mild form as anxiety, worry, and "think, think, think," and in the extreme as "Chicken Little."

Here's a worksheet that can help you discover whether you are operating primarily from the gut, heart, or head (or some combination of them).

3 PEARLS SELF-AWARENESS WORKSHEET

Scale each item and reflect on the <u>overall</u> description of each TRIAD.

0 = Not true at all. 10 = Always true.

	/10	**HEART** - I move and feel moved mostly by my feelings. When I walk into a room, I usually first emotionally connect with how I relate to others to determine my next action.
2	/10	**SELF-EXAGGERATION** - If I reflect, I think I am unconsciously aware of how I am exaggerating aspects of myself and hiding others. I often have a heartfelt longing for my wholeness to be seen.
3	/10	**HOW CAN I BE SEEN?** If I reflect, I am often very aware of how I'm being seen by others. I tend to project a self-image to feel good about myself and get what I need from others.
4	/10	**WORTH CONTINUUM** - Under pressure, my default reaction is usually a mix of: • At a softer volume it could express as feeling embarrassed, less than, or masked. • At a louder volume it could manifest as pride, vanity, shame, or even self-contempt.
		TOTAL

	/10	**HEAD** - I move and feel moved mostly by my thinking. When I walk into a room, I usually first use my mind to consider things and determine my next move.
5	/10	**PERCEPTION OF SEPARATENESS** - If I reflect, I am aware of how I carry an unconscious perception of separateness. A clear type of mental dividing and polarizing. A categorizing and compartmentalizing of life.
6	/10	**HOW CAN I BE SAFE AND SECURE?** If I reflect, I am often unconsciously checking in with how secure I feel. My thoughts seek ways to manage this by searching for answers to calm my concerns.
7	/10	**FEAR CONTINUUM** - Under pressure, my default reaction is usually a mix of: • At a softer volume it could express as anxiety, "think, think, think," and worry. • At a louder volume it could manifest as dread, panic, "Chicken Little," horror, or even terror. **TOTAL**

	/10	**GUT** - I move and feel moved mostly by a gut feel of things. When I walk into a room, I usually rely mostly on my instincts to determine my next action.
8	/10	**RESISTING REALITY** - If I reflect, I seem to have an underlying unconscious resistance to reality. An underlying "Grrr." An initial gut-based pushing back at life and my experiences.
9	/10	**HOW CAN I IMPACT?** If I reflect, I am often unconsciously aware of how I am being impacted and how I am impacting my world. I feel it in my body and its reaction to the situation.
1	/10	**ANGER CONTINUUM** - Under pressure, my default reaction is usually a mix of: • At a softer volume it could express as irritation, grumpiness, or aggravation. • At a louder volume it could manifest as passion, rage, wrath, or even fury.
		TOTAL

Now on to the nine Polarities that sit within those three colored triads, or Pearls.

The good news is that that the Polarities (the nine "types") are easy to recognize and relate to. You will probably be able to identify different Polarities among your close friends, family, and colleagues. Don't put too much weight on the "name" of each Polarity—some sound loftier and more aspirational than others. (After all, most people want to be helpers and achievers, but not all are fundamentally driven by this need.) Some of my clients prefer to rename each of the Polarities as someone they are familiar with so they can really envision and remember it.

The bad news is that it can seem complex at first glance. The richness of information behind the arrows representing influence under conditions of security (the arrows pointing in both directions to/from the Polarity type) and under conditions of stress (the arrow pointing toward the Polarity type) can be confusing at first. There are also "wings" that lie on either side of a Polarity, one of which is typically more heavily weighted.

ENNEAGRAM SUMMARY

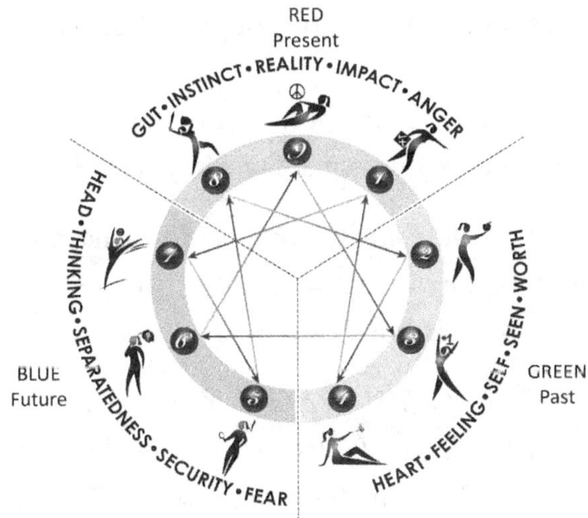

Just to add to the confusion: some individuals modulate their approaches and style as they grow; and some people (while in the moment of taking the assessment) can be primarily under conditions of stress or of security. This can generate an assessment that suggests multiple possibilities for the individual's Polarity. At this point it's tempting to think "*Well, that doesn't enlighten me much!*" and throw it in the trash bin. Take the time to explore it, even if it might seem useless at first glance.

The most enlightening approach to realizing the richness of the Enneagram is to explore it with a Certified Enneagram Coach (which I am—see contact info at the end).

That being said, multiple assessments are available online (of varying quality and cost). My recommendation is to go to the original Enneagram Institute source:

www.EnneagramInstitute.com

Take the "RHETI" assessment, which has 144 questions. The fee at the time of this writing is $15. It takes about 30 to 40 minutes to complete and will then provide you with an output report and a more detailed description of the top couple of Polarities you identify with.

If you want to dig deeper, there is a ton of literature out there about the Enneagram. My personal favorites are:

- *The Wisdom of the Enneagram* by Don Richard Riso and Russ Hudson. It explores the nine personality types and their psychological and spiritual growth.

- *Understand Yourself, Understand Your Partner: The Essential Enneagram Guide to a Better Relationship* by Jennifer Schneider and Ron Corn. It describes the relationship dynamics between pairings and can provide invaluable insight into any co-parenting relationship as you enter a new phase of your partnership lives.

What follows is my take on each Polarity as a one-page description. All pages are formatted the same and include:

- A figurine that captures the essence of the Polarity

- A list of descriptive words on the left (with the generally more appealing ones at the top, the generally less flattering ones below)

- A guide to other Polarities accessed under conditions of security or stress at the bottom.

Remember that your "wing" lies on either side of your number (e.g., the number to the left or to the right of you in the circle).

I realize it's less informative to read alone than to discuss, but hopefully this gets you started.

As they say at Nike, "*Just do it!*" (Learn and explore your Enneagram type.)

What follows are the nine one-pagers (and for you logical types, don't ask me why the numbers start with 2, with 1 at the end. I've often wondered about that and wanted to rotate the whole thing myself, but alas, that would totally confuse things!).

GREEN

I'm trying to be **helpful**

Giving

Nurture

You

Love

Connect

Kind

Warm

Hero

Yes

Hostess

Charming

Pleasing

Proud

Sentimental

Flattery

Sensitive

Possessive

Martyr

You Are Possible

GREEN

*I'm trying to be the **best***

Success

Win, 1st

Action

Competitive

Faster

Visible

Star

Me

Network

Entrepreneurial

Yes

Outdo

Flattery

Entertain

Show-off

Vain

Self-promote

Self-serving

Arrogant

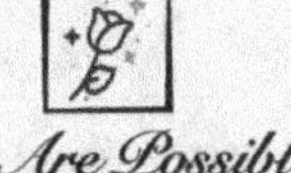

You Are Possible

GREEN

I'm trying to be <u>unique</u>

Different

Original

Unique

New

Me

Self-expression

Creative

Flair

Deep

Outsider

Feelings

Sensitive

Wounded

Strange

Moody

Drama

Dramatic

You Are Possible

4 The Individualist

BLUE

HEAD•THINKING•SEPARATEDNESS•SECURITY•FEAR

I'm trying to **understand**

Understand

Know

Learn

Observe

Focus

Watch

Detach

Intense

Alone

Isolated

Bookworm

Cool

Aloof

Ivory tower

Hermit

You Are Possible

BLUE

I'm trying to feel **secure**

Question

Solve

Maybe

What if?

Diligent

Plan

Test

Check

Discern

Feedback

Defend

Support

Protect

Unsure

Cautious

Doubt

Worry

Chicken Little

You Are Possible

BLUE

The Enthusiast

I'm trying to be __happy__

Energy

Alive

Happy

Positive

Imagination

Dream

Freedom

Possibilities

Social

YOLO

Play

New

Adventure

Dare me

Scattered

Unfocused

FOMO

Wild

Unreliable

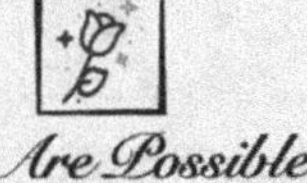

You Are Possible

RED

I'm trying to be **strong**

Lead
Presence
Strategy
Focus
Resourceful
Now
Direct
Decisive
Respect
Power
Loyalty
My will
My way or highway
Command
Challenge
Revenge
War
Ruthless

You Are Possible

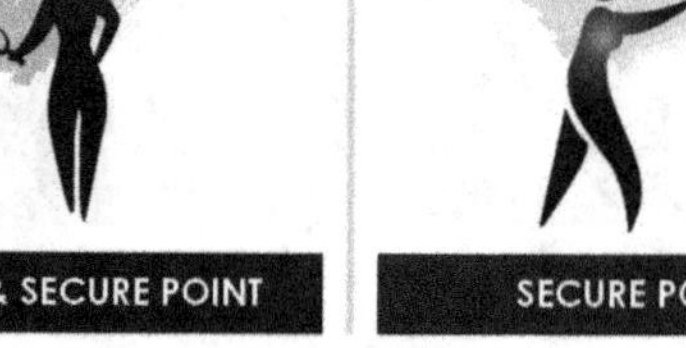

RED

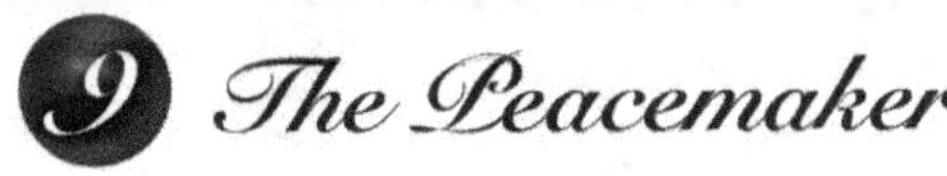

I'm trying to be **peaceful**

Peace
Go with the flow
Patient
Self-effacing
Nice
Merge
Kind
Neutral
OK
Chilled
Dreamer
Invisible
Numb
Avoid
Not now
Tuned out
Slow
Denial
Boiling point

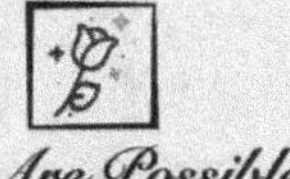

You Are Possible

9 The Peacemaker

RED

(There, see, Polarity 1 eventually shows up!)

If you are still struggling with discovering your type, here's a worksheet that can help guide your thinking around which Polarity you are growing from. Have fun and explore! Even better, discuss the nuances with an Enneagram Coach, or pick up the books I mentioned at the beginning of this chapter.

9 POLARITIES SELF-AWARENESS WORKSHEET

Scale each and reflect on the <u>overall</u> description of each POLARITY.

0 = Not true at all. 10 = Always true.

2 /10	I'm trying to be seen as <u>helpful</u>. I'm trying not to be seen as **selfish**.	I am a <u>helper.</u> I place **your needs** above my needs. I do **a lot for others**, and I work hard to be seen as **kind** rather than unkind. I'm **proud** to be your ideal someone, instead of being humbly real. To **give** is easier than to receive, **even at my expense**. I can pretend **"I'm okay"** instead of being emotionally honest.
3 /10	I'm trying to be seen as the **best**. I'm trying not to be seen as a **loser**.	I am an <u>achiever</u>. By **winning** I avoid the pain of losing. I say "Yes, **I can**" rather than admit "No, I can't." Let's deliver results **fast** rather than slow. I can **wing it** and **make it happen** rather than engage in tedious learning. I can show a **facade of success** to hide fear of failure. Let's **show** that I can **solve** this problem **quick**. I can **burn out**.
4 /10	I'm trying to be seen as <u>unique</u>. I'm trying not to be seen as	I am an <u>individualist</u>. I'd rather be a **dysfunctional outsider** than a functional sheep. **My emotional needs** are above your emotional needs. It's all about **me**, not you. I feel things **deeply** rather than objectively. My **emotions** feel like facts. I prefer **drama** to reality.
5 /10	I'm trying to <u>understand</u>. I'm trying not to lack	I am an <u>investigator</u>. One can never have enough **knowledge** to remove ignorance. I feel **safer** when **isolated** rather than engaged. I can **hide in my mind** to avoid my heart. It's **easier to observe** than participate. I strive for **competency** in life and fear incompetence.
6 /10	I'm trying to feel **secure**. I'm trying not to **lose support**.	I am a **thinker**. I seek **information** and **truth** and ask a lot of **questions**. I'd rather **overplan** than risk being underprepared. I fear deceit. Should I **trust or doubt**? **Fairness** is important and I speak bravely against **unfairness**. Am I with **us or them**? I'm sensitive to the **underdog** vs. aggressor.
7 /10	I'm trying to be <u>happy</u>. I'm trying not to be **unhappy**.	I am an <u>enthusiast</u>. I chase **fun** and fear boredom. I want **freedom** from feeling trapped. I keep busy to **avoid stillness**. I seek **pleasure** to run from pain. I keep many **possibilities** open to **avoid limitation**. I **dream** of a **happy future** rather than focus on the realities of the present.
8 /10	I'm trying to be **strong**. I'm trying not to be **weak**.	I am a <u>challenger</u>. I take **control** rather than submit. I choose **war** and I don't easily surrender. I want **power** to not feel powerless. It's **my way or the highway**. **Revenge** is better than forgiveness. **Honor** me, and never be disloyal to me. I **own** rather than share or give.
9 /10	I'm trying to be **peaceful**. I'm trying not to disturb the **peace**.	I am a <u>peacemaker</u>. It's often easier to **tune out** rather than be fully awake. I prefer to take my time **slowly** rather than be very dynamic. It's **better to avoid** rather than confront. I can **numb** instead of asserting myself. It's easier to **hide** than show up, **follow** than lead. **But when pushed, I pounce.**
1 /10	I'm trying to be **good**. I'm trying not to be **bad**.	I am a <u>reformer</u>. I appreciate and **follow the rules**. There's only **right or wrong**. It's **black or white**; there is no gray. I'm striving for **perfect** and struggle with imperfection. I have very **high standards**, and don't tolerate low standards. I tend to be **hyperresponsible**, not irresponsible. I expect others to follow the rules and **let them know it**.

My Enneagram Type:

____

My Stress Point:

____

My Secure Points:

____

My Wing(s):

____

B. CLIFTON STRENGTHS

Clifton Strengths (owned by Gallup, created and developed by Don Clifton) builds on who you *already are*, as opposed to highlighting and focusing on overcoming deficits or challenges.

It identifies 34 Themes (or most common talents) and has a chapter describing each one:

Achiever	Activator	Adaptability
Analytical	Arranger	Belief
Command	Communication	Competition
Connectedness	Consistency	Context
Deliberative	Developer	Discipline
Empathy	Focus	Futuristic
Harmony	Ideation	Includer
Individualization	Input	Intellection
Learner	Maximizer	Positivity
Relator	Responsibility	Restorative
Self-Assurance	Significance	Strategic

WOO! *(You'll have to take the test to decipher that one for yourself.)*

The book is available on Amazon ($18 at the time of this writing). It describes each Strength in 34 short (1–2 page) chapters and includes a personal code to take the online assessment (which will take you about 15 minutes). That's another quick and inexpensive investment in your own understanding of you!

Strengthsfinder 2.0 from Gallup: Discover Your Clifton Strengths

If you choose to take the assessment, I challenge you to think about these three questions as they relate to your impending leave and transition back to work:

- What are your top strengths to leverage?

- How have you been leveraging them?

- How are you going to leverage them going forward, and specifically upon your return to your career?

My Top 5 Clifton Strengths:

1. ____

2. ____

3. ____

4. ____

5. ____

C. MYERS-BRIGGS (MBTI)

If you've been around the corporate world for a while, it's highly likely that you've encountered and probably even taken the "Myers-Briggs" (aka "MBTI" or Myers-Briggs Type Indicator) assessment at some point.

It identifies 16 "Types" which are derived from four forces, each of which has two pairs (E vs. I, S vs. N, T vs. F, and J vs. P).

1. *Source of Energy*: Extraversion or Introversion

2. *Information-Gathering Function*: Sensing or iNtuition

3. *Decision-Making Function*: Thinking or Feeling

4. *Lifestyle Orientation*: Judging or Perceiving

While it can be highly useful in understanding our behaviors and that of others, I find that it can be challenging to keep track of and understand all 16 types (other than my own ENTJ type, which of course I find most interesting and worthy of deep study).

So, in my sometimes-simplistic mind, I've developed a couple of overview/cheat sheet summaries, which are largely modified from a wonderful book, *Type Talk* by Otto Kroeger and Janet M. Thuesen.

If you don't already know your four-letter type, an online assessment is available at www.mbtionline.com. It's approved by the Myers-Briggs Foundation and at the time of this writing it is $49.95 for the assessment and read-out report. It takes less than an hour and can be quite insightful and helpful.

Here's the highest-level summary of the way I think about MBTI (largely derived from the *Type Talk* book mentioned above).

MYERS-BRIGGS KEY DIMENSIONS

E or I?	**Extraversion** • Focus on the outer world. • Energy by interacting with people and/or doing things.	**Introversion** • Focus on the inner world. • Energy through reflecting on ideas, information, and/or concepts.
S or N?	**Sensing** • Notice and trust facts, details, and present realities.	**Intuition** • Attend to and trust interrelationships, theories, and future possibilities.
T or F?	**Thinking** • Make decisions using logical analysis to achieve objectivity.	**Feeling** • Make decisions using personality-centered values to achieve harmony.
J or P?	**Judging** • Tend to be organized and orderly and to make decisions quickly.	**Perceiving** • Tend to be flexible and adaptable and to keep options open for as long as possible.

And here's a bit more color around each of the dimensions (again, largely derived from *Type Talk*).

Source of Energy
Extraverts vs. *Introverts*

E Extraversion		I Introversion
Sociability	⟷	Territoriality
Interaction	⟷	Concentration
External	⟷	Internal
Breadth	⟷	Depth
Extensive	⟷	Intensive
Multiple relationships	⟷	Limited relationships
Energy expenditure	⟷	Energy conservation
External events	⟷	Internal reactions
Gregarious	⟷	Reflective
Speak, then think	⟷	Think, then speak

Information-Gathering Function
Sensors vs *iNtuitives*

S Sensing		N Intuition
Sequential	⟷	Random
Present	⟷	Future
Realistic	⟷	Conceptual
Perspiration	⟷	Inspiration
Actual	⟷	Theoretical
Down-to-earth	⟷	Head-in-clouds
Fact	⟷	Fantasy
Practicality	⟷	Ingenuity
Specific	⟷	General

Decision-Making Function
*T*hinkers vs. *F*eelers

T Thinking		F Feeling
Objective	⟵⟶	Subjective
Firm-minded	⟵⟶	Fair-hearted
Laws	⟵⟶	Circumstances
Firmness	⟵⟶	Persuasion
Just	⟵⟶	Humane
Clarity	⟵⟶	Harmony
Critique	⟵⟶	Appreciate
Policy	⟵⟶	Social values
Detached	⟵⟶	Involved

Lifestyle Orientation
*J*udgers vs. *P*erceivers

J Judging		P Perceiving
Resolved	⟵⟶	Pending
Decided	⟵⟶	Wait and see
Fixed	⟵⟶	Flexible
Control	⟵⟶	Adapt
Closure	⟵⟶	Openness
Planned	⟵⟶	Open-ended
Structure	⟵⟶	Flow
Definite	⟵⟶	Tentative
Scheduled	⟵⟶	Spontaneous
Deadline	⟵⟶	What deadline?

Finally, pulling it all together, here's the matrix of all 16 types and some high-level descriptors about how each type might stereotypically present itself.

MYERS-BRIGGS 16 TYPES

		S		N	
		T	F	T	F
I	J	ISTJ "Doing what should be done"	ISFJ "A high sense of duty"	INTJ "Everything has room for improvement"	INFJ "An inspiration to others"
	P	ISTP "Ready to try anything once"	ISFP "Sees much but shares little"	INTP "A love of problem-solving"	INFP "Performing noble service to aid society"
E	J	ESTJ "Life's administrators"	ESFJ "Hosts and hostesses of the world"	ENTJ "Life's natural leaders"	ENFJ "Smooth-talking persuaders"
	P	ESTP "The ultimate realists"	ESFP "You only go around once in life"	ENTP "One exciting challenge after another"	ENFP "Giving life an extra squeeze"

Enjoy, and explore. Read about yourself, read about others. Then tuck it in your tool kit of information about yourself and your interactions with other Types.

My Myers-Briggs Type Indicator (MBTI):

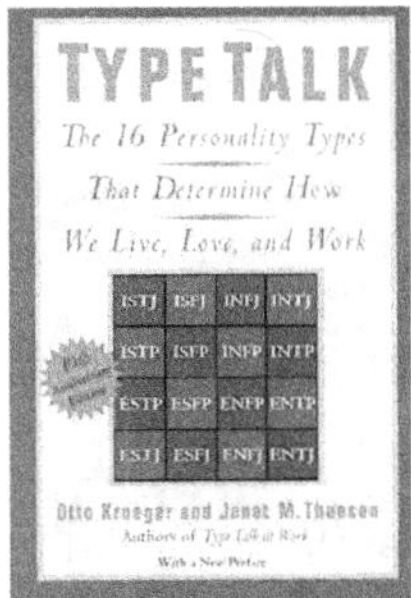

Here's a great book that goes into more detail, available on Amazon.

D. DiSC

Now that we've waded into the Enneagram, Clifton Strengths, and Myers-Briggs, let me share my fourth (and final!) favored assessment tool—DiSC. (Yes, the "i" is not capitalized, and my curious mind had to know why. It turns out they couldn't get the trademark for DISC, so they went with DiSC.

DiSC is commonly explored with working teams, to help reveal and simplify the dynamics of team interactions. There are four primary Styles (green, yellow, red, blue), and at times a secondary Style for each individual. Often, a team plots each member's "dot" on the circle in the appropriate location and team dynamics are explored.

Take a look at the overview below and see if you can "plot" your dot on the circle. Many people can easily recognize their Style. If you are struggling to "plot the dot," you can of course take an online assessment. It becomes even more interesting if you have your whole team take the assessment, which produces an often feisty debate about appropriate team dynamics. There are plenty of good books about DiSC out there to explore.

For you, for now (as you ponder your approach to leaving and returning to work), tuck it into your personal knowledge tool kit.

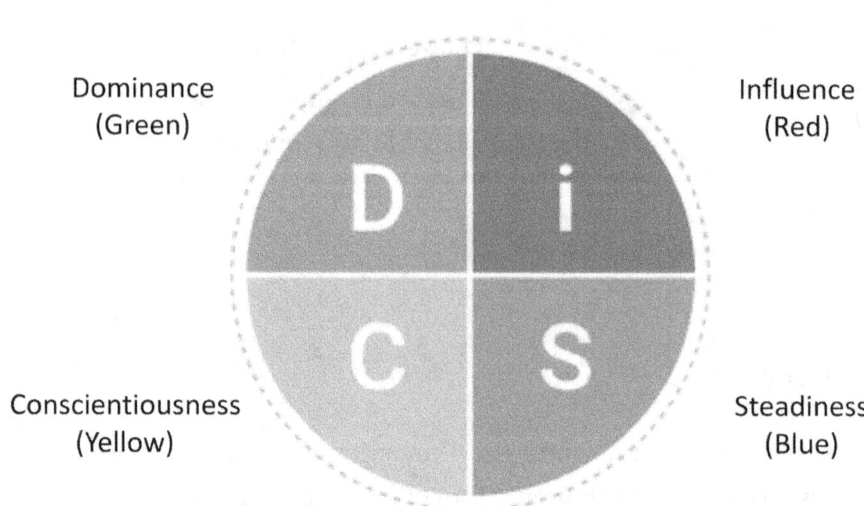

DiSC OVERVIEW

DOMINANCE (Green)	INFLUENCE (Red)
Results **Action** **Challenge** *Motivators*: Power, authority, success, competition, and winning *Values*: Competency, concrete results, personal freedom *Style*: Driven, direct, decisive, strong-willed, self-confident, daring, determined, fast-paced *Fears*: Loss of control, being taken advantage of, vulnerability	**Enthusiasm** **Action** **Collaboration** *Motivators*: Social recognition, group activities, relationships *Values*: Coaching & counseling, freedom of expression, individuality *Style*: Charming, collaborative, energizing, trusting, enthusiastic, impulsive, optimistic, persuasive *Fears*: Social rejection, disapproval, loss of influence, being ignored
CONSCIENTIOUSNESS (Yellow)	**STEADINESS (Blue)**
Accuracy **Stability** **Challenge** *Motivators*: Opportunities to gain knowledge, showing their expertise, quality work *Values*: Quality, accuracy, challenge *Style*: Cautious, systematic, private, objective, analytical, diplomatic, accurate, reserved *Fears*: Criticism, unclear methods, being wrong	**Support** **Stability** **Collaboration** *Motivators*: Cooperation, opportunities to help, sincere appreciation *Values*: Loyalty, helping others, security *Style*: Calm, patient, predictable, deliberate, stable, warm, passive, loyal *Fears*: Loss of stability or harmony, change, offending others

My DiSC Type:

Primary:

____

Secondary:

____

Mindset Matters

In this chapter we will explore our emotions and how to identify them. Then we'll look at those annoying, critical voices in our head—our Saboteurs.

From there, we will look at our negative thoughts and fears.

And we'll explore reframing our mind to one of open, interactive learning, and making distinctions that reframe our thinking.

    A. Emotions: Name Them to Tame Them

    B. Saboteurs and Sages

    C. ANTs

    D. FEAR

    E. Open vs. Closed Minds

    F. Distinctions That Reframe

A. EMOTIONS: NAME THEM TO TAME THEM

Emotions are pesky little things, and tons of books out there go into them in depth (written by psychologists who have way more expertise on this topic than me). Each framework seems to convey its own nuances and classifications. I don't think any one framework is better than any other.

My point is that we often skirt over emotions (unless they are glaringly unpleasant) and bury them.

Pause to really feel and answer: *"How are you (feeling)?"* (And not in the casual passing of someone in the hall, superficial kind of way). This goes a long way toward building our self-awareness and inner resilience. Here is one of my favorites (or pick another off the Web that might better resonate with you). Make it a daily habit to check in with yourself. Get clear on how you *feel* and what *emotions* are driving it.

Emotions Wheel

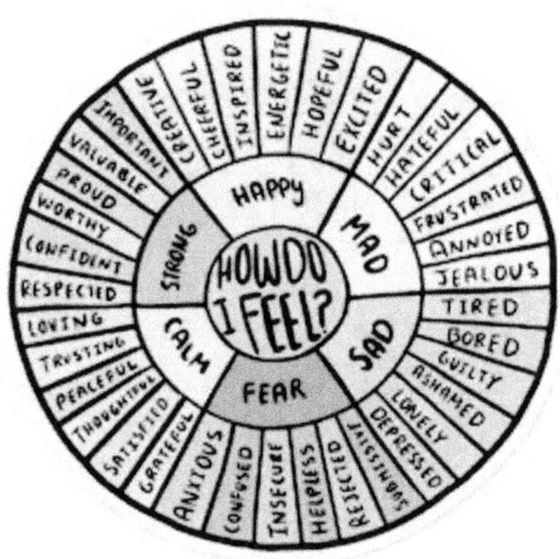

Emotions are what we FEEL. Not who we ARE.

Skillfully manage your thoughts and emotions so they don't manage you!

B. SABOTEURS AND SAGES

The basic idea here is to become aware of our "Saboteurs" and tame them by unleashing our "Sages." There's a lot of depth to this research and thinking. If you want the detail, there's a great book titled *Positive Intelligence*, by Shirzad Chamine. At the time of writing the hard copy of this book was wickedly expensive (perhaps they ran out of books?), but the e-versions were reasonably priced and readily available.

OPPOSING FORCES OF SABOTEURS AND SAGES

Saboteurs	*Sages*
Deliberately destroy, damage, or obstruct (something or someone)	Have a profoundly wise manner

Recent advances in functional MRI (fMRI) have enabled us (well, technically, other people) to pinpoint the regions of the brain involved in producing thoughts and feelings, and identify the neural functions involved with what can be called Saboteurs and Sages.

The Saboteurs: Live in the brainstem, limbic system, and parts of the left brain, generating negative emotions while you handle life's challenges. They produce much of our stress, anxiety, self-doubt, anger, shame, guilt, frustration, and negative mind chatter! They present in 10 forms:

- Judge (this one is universal—we all have one)

- Avoider

- Controller

- Hyper-achiever

- Hyper-rational

- Hyper-vigilant

- Pleaser

- Restless

- Stickler

- Victim

The Sages: Live in the middle prefrontal cortex "empathy circuitry" and parts of the right brain, generating positive emotions while handling life's challenges. Activating this region releases endorphins, which support feelings of empathy, compassion, gratitude, curiosity, joy of creativity, and calm, clear-headed, laser-focused action. They present in 5 forms:

- Activate

- Empathize

- Explore

- Innovate

- Navigate

There's a free online self-evaluation that helps highlight what your Saboteurs might be (courtesy of Shirzad Chamine). It can add another layer of insight into who we are and how we're wired, and that is worth exploring. I think you will be amazed by becoming aware of where all that incessant self-chatter is coming from throughout the day. See PositiveIntelligence.com.

Meanwhile, here's my take on each of the Saboteurs. We all have all of them, just in varying degrees of obnoxious loudness. If you watch for them, you will recognize them talking in your head—incessantly and loudly and rudely. If our best friend spoke to us as our Saboteurs do, you'd likely never speak with them again. Seriously.

Flip through the one-page descriptions of each of the Saboteurs, and rate each for yourself on a scale of 1–10. Then identify the ones that attack you the most strongly and most often. These are the voices we must become acutely aware of and tame, particularly as they cast doubt on your return-to-work decision and approach. Pick one or two to pay attention to and don't let them get to you and sap your confidence!

Let's start with The Judge, our universal Saboteur.

 ## Saboteur: The Judge   __ / 10

THE JUDGE

Finds faults with self, others, and circumstances. Causes much of our disappointment, anger, regret, guilt, shame, and anxiety. Activates other Saboteurs.

Characteristics

- <u>Self</u>: Badgers self for past mistakes or current shortcomings

- <u>Others</u>: Focuses on what is wrong with others rather than appreciating the good things about them. Gets into inferior/superior comparisons.

- <u>Circumstances</u>: Insists a circumstance or outcome is "bad" rather than seeing it as a gift and opportunity

Thoughts

- *"What is wrong with me?"*
- *"What is wrong with you?"*
- *"What is wrong with this?"*

Feelings

- All of our guilt, regret, shame, and disappointment
- Much of our anxiety and anger

Justification Lies

- "Without pushing you, you'll get lazy."
- "Without punishing you for mistakes, you won't learn."
- "Without scaring you about bad outcomes you won't work hard to prevent them."
- "Without judging others, you'll lose objectivity and not protect your self-interest."
- "Without making you feel bad, you won't change."

Impact (on self and others)

- Guilt, regret, shame, disappointment, anxiety, and anger
- Relationship conflicts

Adapted from: *Positive Intelligence,* Shirzad Chamine

And now let's take a peek at the 9 Accomplice Saboteurs! Recognize these in yourself?!

 ## Saboteur: The Avoider

___ / 10

AVOIDER

A focus on the positive and pleasant in an extreme way.

An avoidance of difficult and unpleasant tasks and conflicts.

Characteristics

- Avoids conflict
- Says "yes" when not desired
- Downplays problems
- Deflects to others
- Has difficulty saying "no"
- Passive-aggressive behaviors
- Loses self in comforting routines and habits
- Procrastinates

Thoughts

- "This is just too unpleasant."
- "Maybe if I let it go it will take care of itself."
- "I'll hurt someone's feelings and I'd rather not."
- "I don't like conflict."
- "I've found balance and I don't want to mess with it."
- "I don't want to create a scene."

Feelings

- Tries to remain even keeled
- Feels anxiety about the avoidance or procrastination
- Fears interruption of hard-earned peace of mind

Justification Lies

- "It's good to spare others' feelings."
- "No good comes out of conflict."
- "If you can't say something nice, say nothing at all."
- "It's good to be flexible."
- "Someone needs to be the peacemaker."
- "You catch 'em better with sugar."

Impact (on self and others)

- What's avoided doesn't go away. It festers.
- Relationships are superficial through conflict avoidance.
- Others' trust is eroded because it's unclear when negative information is withheld.
- Authenticity erodes by denying conflicts and negativities.

Adapted from: *Positive Intelligence,* Shirzad Chamine

Saboteur: The Controller

_ / 10

Characteristics

- Strong need to control and take charge
- Connects through competition, challenge, physicality, or conflict
- Willful, confrontational straight talker
- Comes alive when doing the impossible
- Stimulated by and connects through conflict
- Intimidates others
- In-your-face communication interpreted as anger or criticism

Thoughts

- *"I am either in control or out of control."*
- *"If I work hard enough, I can and should control the situation to go my way."*
- *"Others want and need me to take control."*
- *"No one tells me what to do."*

Feelings

- Anxious when something not going their way
- Angry and intimidating when others don't follow
- Impatient with others' feelings and different styles
- Does feel hurt and rejected, though rarely admits to it

Justification Lies

- *"Without me, you can't get much done."*
- *"You need to push people."*
- *"If I don't control, I will be controlled."*
- *"I am trying to get the job done for all our sakes."*

Impact (on self and others)

- Gets temporary results
- Generates anxiety in others who feel controlled, resentful, manipulated, and unable to tap into their own value
- Generates anxiety in self as most things are ultimately not controllable

Adapted from: *Positive Intelligence*, Shirzad Chamine

Saboteur: The Hyper-achiever

`_ / 10`

HYPER-ACHIEVER

Dependent on constant performance and achievement for self-respect and self-validation.

Highly focused on external success, leading to workaholic tendencies and loss of touch with deeper emotional and relationship needs.

Characteristics

- Competitive
- Image- and status-conscious
- Good at covering up insecurities and projecting a positive image
- Adapts personality to fit what impresses others
- Goal-oriented, workaholic tendencies
- More drawn to perfecting public image than introspection
- Can be self-promoting
- Keeps people at a safe distance

Thoughts

- "I must be the best at what I do."
- "If I can't be outstanding, don't bother trying."
- "I must be efficient and effective."
- "Emotions get in the way of performance."
- "Focus on thinking and action."
- "I can be anything I want to be."
- "I am worthy and successful because others think so."

Feelings

- Doesn't like to dwell on feelings too long
- Sometimes feels empty and depressed inside
- Needs to feel successful
- Feels worthy mainly through accomplishment
- May fear intimacy and vulnerability as closeness might reveal imperfections

Justification Lies

- "Life is about achieving and perfecting results."
- "Portraying a great image is what helps me get results."
- "Feelings are just a distraction and don't achieve much."

Impact (on self and others)

- Peace and happiness are short-lived in brief celebrations of achievement.
- Self-acceptance is continuously dependent on the next success.
- Loses touch with deeper feelings and self
- Has difficulty connecting intimately with others
- Can pull others into the lopsided performance vortex

Adapted from: *Positive Intelligence, Shirzad Chamine*

Saboteur: The Hyper-rational

_ / 10

Characteristics

- Intense and active mind
- Can come across as intellectually arrogant or secretive
- Private, doesn't let many people into deeper feelings

- Mostly shows feelings through passion for ideas
- Prefers to watch and analyze from a distance
- Can lose track of time due to intense concentration
- Strong penchant for skepticism and debate

Thoughts

- *"The rational mind is where it's at."*
- *"Feelings are distracting and irrelevant."*
- *"Many people are irrational and sloppy thinkers."*
- *"Needs and emotions of others distract me."*
- *"I need to shut out intrusions."*
- *"Knowledge, understanding, and insight are the most valuable."*

Feelings

- Frustrated with others being emotional and irrational
- Anxious about preserving personal time, energy, and resources against intrusion
- Can feels different, alone, or misunderstood
- Is often skeptical or cynical

Justification Lies

- *"A rational mind is the best mind."*
- *"I have to protect myself from other people's wasteful intrusion."*
- *"Other people's messy emotions and needs slow my work down."*

Impact (on self and others)

- Limits the depth and flexibility of relationships
- Spends time analyzing rather than experiencing feelings and life
- Intimidates less analytically minded people

Adapted from: *Positive Intelligence*, Shirzad Chamine

 Saboteur: The Hyper-vigilant __ / 10

Characteristics

- Always anxious, with chronic doubts about self and others
- Extraordinary sensitivity to danger signals
- Constant expectation of mishap or danger

- Suspicious of what others are up to
- Expectation that others will mess up
- May seek reassurance and guidance in procedures, rules, authorities, and institutions

Thoughts

- *"When is the other shoe going to drop?"*
- *"If I make a mistake, everyone will jump down my throat."*
- *"I want to trust people, but I am suspicious of their motives."*
- *"I need to know the rules, even if I don't always follow them."*

Feelings

- Skeptical
- Sometimes cynical
- Often anxious
- Always highly vigilant

Justification Lies

- *"Life is full of dangers."*
- *"If I don't look out for danger, who will?"*
- *"Someone will get hurt if I don't watch out for them."*

Impact (on self and others)

- Burns vital energy that could otherwise be put to great use
- Loses credibility with "the boy who cried wolf" phenomenon
- Others feel drained by the intensity of the nervous energy, and may avoid interaction.

 # Saboteur: The Pleaser

__ / 10

PLEASER

Indirectly attempts to gain acceptance and affection by helping, pleasing, rescuing, or flattering others.

Loses sight of own needs and becomes resentful as a result.

Characteristics

- Strong need to be liked
- Earns being liked by helping, pleasing, rescuing, or flattering others
- Needs frequent reassurance of the acceptance and affection of others
- Doesn't express own needs openly and directly
- Indirectly expresses own needs by making people feel obligated to reciprocate

Thoughts

- *"A good person puts the needs of others ahead of their own."*
- *"People can be so selfish and ungrateful when they don't notice or care about what I've done."*
- *"I give to others too much, but not to myself."*
- *"I can get anyone to like me."*
- *"If I don't help rescue them, no one else will."*

Feelings

- Expressing own needs directly feels selfish
- Worried that insisting on own ideas will drive others away
- Resents being taken for granted, but has difficulty expressing it

Justification Lies

- *"I don't do this for myself, I do it for others."*
- *"I help others selflessly and don't expect anything in return."*
- *"The world would be better if everyone behaved like me."*

Impact (on self and others)

- Can jeopardize taking care of one's own needs (emotional, physical, or financial)
- Can lead to resentment and burnout
- Others can develop dependence instead of learning to take care of themselves.
- Others can feel obligated, guilty, or manipulated.

Adapted from: *Positive Intelligence, Shirzad Chamine*

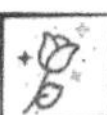 # Saboteur: The Restless

`__ / 10`

RESTLESS

Constantly in search of greater excitement in the next activity and constantly busy.

Rarely at peace or content with the current activity.

Characteristics

- Easily distracted
- Can get scattered
- Stays busy, juggling tasks and plans
- Seeks excitement and variety, not comfort and safety
- Bounces (escapes) from unpleasant feelings very quickly
- Seeks constant new stimulation

Thoughts

- *"This isn't very fulfilling."*
- *"The next thing has got to be more exciting."*
- *"Negative feelings suck so I move on to the next thing."*
- *"No one seems to be able to keep up with me."*

Feelings

- Impatient with what's happening in the present
- Wonders what's next
- Fears missing out on more worthwhile experiences
- Feels restless and wants more options
- Worries that focus on a negative feeling would make it grow and become overwhelming

Justification Lies

- *"Life is too short, and should be lived fully."*
- *"I don't want to miss out – FOMO!"*

Impact (on self and others)

- Anxiety-based escape from being present is underneath a surface of fun and excitement.
- Avoids real and lasting focus on the issues and relationships that truly matter
- Others have a hard time keeping up with the frenzy and chaos, and are unable to build a sustainable relationship.

Adapted from: *Positive Intelligence*, Shirzad Chamine

 Saboteur: The Stickler   __ / 10

STICKLER

Perfection and a need for order and organization taken too far.

Characteristics

- Perfectionist, punctual, methodical
- Highly critical of self and others
- Can be irritable, tense, opinionated, sarcastic
- Strong need for self-control and self-restraint
- Works overtime to make up for others' sloppiness or laziness
- Is highly sensitive to criticism

Thoughts

- *"I know the right way."*
- *"If you can't do it well, don't do it at all."*
- *"Others have really lax standards."*
- *"I need to be more organized and methodical than others so that things get done."*
- *"I hate mistakes."*
- *"I hate wasting time."*

Feelings

- Constant disappointment and frustration with self and others for not living up to high standards
- Anxious that others will mess up the balance and order
- Sarcastic, with self-righteous overtones
- Suppressed anger and frustration

Justification Lies

- *"It's a personal obligation."*
- *"It's up to me to fix the messes I encounter."*
- *"Perfectionism is good."*
- *"When things are good, I feel better about myself"*
- *"There's usually a clear right and wrong way and I know how it should be done."*
- *"I've got to do the right thing."*

Impact (on self and others)

- Causes rigidity and reduces flexibility in interacting with change and the diverse styles of others
- Is a source of ongoing anxiety and frustration
- Causes resentment, anxiety, self-doubt, and resignation in others who feel continually criticized
- Others resign themselves to the fact that no matter how hard they try, the Stickler will not be pleased.

Adapted from: *Positive Intelligence*, Shirzad Chamine

 Saboteur: The Victim

__ / 10

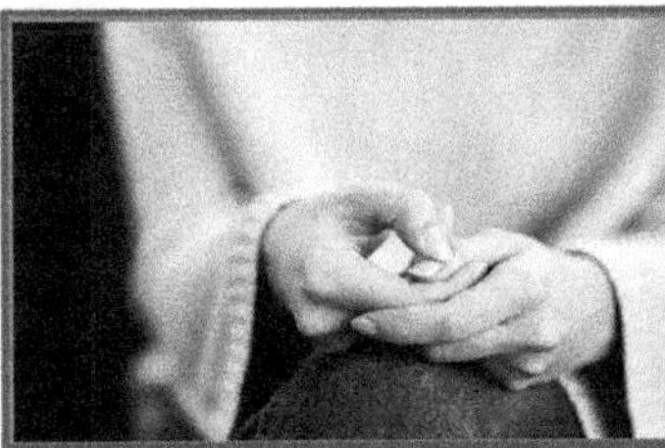

VICTIM

Emotional and temperamental style to gain attention and affection.

An extreme focus on internal feelings, particularly painful ones. A martyr streak.

Characteristics

- If criticized or misunderstood, tends to withdraw, pout and sulk
- Fairly dramatic and temperamental
- When things get tough, wants to crumble and give up
- Represses rage, resulting in depression, apathy, or constant fatigue
- Unconsciously attracted to having difficulties
- Gets attention by having emotional problems, or being temperamental and sullen

Thoughts

- *"No one understands me."*
- *"Poor me. Terrible things always happen to me."*
- *"I might be uniquely disadvantaged."*
- *"I am what I feel."*
- *"I wish someone would rescue me from this mess."*

Feelings

- Tends to brood over negative feelings for a long time
- Feels alone and lonely, even around family and friends
- Experiences feelings of melancholy and abandonment
- Dwells on envy and negative comparisons

Justification Lies

- *"At least when I act this way, I get some of the love and attention I deserve."*
- *"Sadness is noble and sophisticated. It shows exceptional depth, insight, and sensitivity."*
- *"Bad things always happen to me, and I have to cope with it."*

Impact (on self and others)

- Vitality wasted by focus on internal processing and brooding
- Backfires by pushing people away
- Others feel frustrated, helpless, or guilty that they can only put Band-Aids on the Victim's pain.
- Others give up on a two-way relationship and walk away.

Adapted from: *Positive Intelligence*, Shirzad Chamine

Now sum it up for yourself, become aware, and tame the Saboteurs!

WHICH OF YOUR SABOTEURS ARE YOUR BIGGEST ENEMY TO TAME?

Saboteur	Your Self-Score
JUDGE	____
Avoider	____
Controller	____
Hyper-achiever	____
Hyper-rational	____
Hyper-vigilant	____
Pleaser	____
Restless	____
Stickler	____
Victim	____

C. ANTS

Photo credit: Peter F. Wolf, Unsplash.com

ANTs are those pesky, meandering, annoying creatures that crawl all over us. It's also the acronym for Automatic Negative Thoughts (ANTs). For many of us, our natural go-to is the negative.

The doomsday. The horrible possibility. Ah, Chicken Little! While these thoughts might often cross our minds, the trick is first to be aware of them when they surface, and then to nip them in the proverbial bud.

Some questions you might ask yourself to challenge Automatic Negative Thoughts are:

- Is this fact or fiction?

- What is the evidence?

- What data runs counter to this?

- How might someone else see this?

- What advice would I give a person in the same situation?

- What are possibly more realistic and optimistic thoughts?

Many ANTs turn out to be completely unfounded, and those that do have some basis often turn out to be not as bad as we thought—which brings me to the next acronym.

D. FEAR

This is one of my favorite word-expansion acronyms. It's so relevant to me that I should probably have it tattooed on my wrist as a good reminder.

FEAR:
Future
Events
Appearing
Real!

Photo credit: Melody P, Unsplash.com

We certainly can't change the past (though we can learn from it and grow). And we most definitely can't predict the future (or we'd make a trillion dollars being paid to share our knowledge). So, all we have is the present.

For the most part, the present isn't actually all that bad, and certainly nothing to fear (unless you're being attacked by a bear in that very moment).

Yes, most of us possess an uncanny and unhealthy ability to project ourselves into possible (and usually unlikely) future scenarios that have us running around like Chicken Little and imagining what our homeless lives will be like in a cardboard box under the freeway, with no friends at all to be able to take us in. I myself can climb that inference ladder in seconds flat.

So, cut it out! When FEAR creeps in, engage your cognitive brain, ground yourself, and think about what your current reality is.

You'll need a strong dose of this advice as you imagine returning to work! My Top 5 FEAR Ideas:

In life:

____

____

____

____

In work:

____

____

____

____

E. OPEN VS. CLOSED MINDS

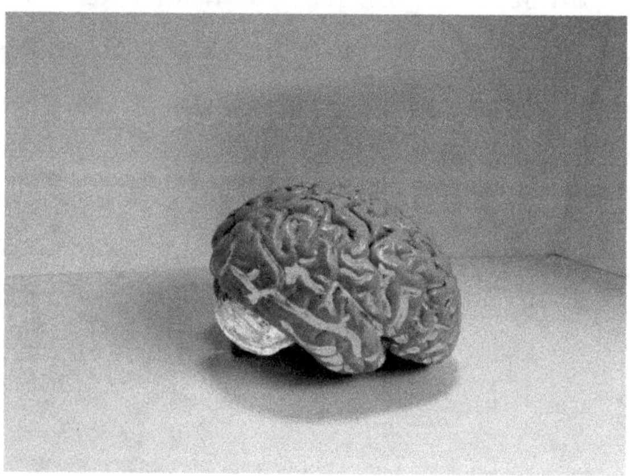

Photo credit: Natasha Connell, Unsplash.com

In the broadest terms, we can be more inclined toward either "open" or "closed" minds.

With a *closed mind*, we believe that our basic qualities (for example, capabilities, skills, intelligence, or talent) are simply fixed traits. We spend our time confirming and proving and documenting our talents, rather than actually developing them. In a closed mind, you'd better be flawless. And perfect.

With an *open mind*, we believe that we can continually develop these qualities. That where we are now is just the starting point for where we can go. In an open mind, we are open to learning and we build resilience. We can even laugh at ourselves and see challenges and setbacks as learning along our journey.

Returning to work will be different from how work was before your bundle of joy arrived. There will be new challenges—and they can be opportunities to grow if you let them.

Here are some ways of thinking about the two different minds.

CLOSED VS. OPEN MINDSETS

Growth:	Static	⟷	Developing
Attitude:	Knower	⟷	Learner
Challenges:	Avoid	⟷	Embrace
Obstacles:	Give up	⟷	Persist
Effort:	Wasteful	⟷	Path to mastery
Criticism:	Ignore	⟷	Learn from
Comparisons:	Feel threatened	⟷	Find inspiration and lessons
Development:	Deterministic	⟷	Free will

F. DISTINCTIONS THAT REFRAME

Words are important. Even the words we use in our own minds.

Sometimes changing a word can make a distinction that shifts how mindful we are in our intent.

Below are some examples of distinctions that reframe our perspectives.

This kind of reframing can be a powerful resource in your tool kit for thinking about leaving and returning to work. Take a moment to circle the one on the left or right side of each double arrow that most describe the way you think about things. Note any distinctions that you want to challenge yourself to reframe. Maybe start with one or two.

DISTINCTIONS THAT REFRAME

Achieving	⟷	Winning	Inner Wisdom	⟷	Inner Critic
Afraid	⟷	Powerless	Intention	⟷	Goal
Belonging	⟷	Fitting in	Leadership	⟷	Management
Both/And	⟷	Either/Or	Mastery	⟷	Perfection
Clarity	⟷	Certainty	Power With	⟷	Power Over
Contributing	⟷	Self-Sacrificing	Self-Care	⟷	Self-Sedating
Effective	⟷	Efficient	Service	⟷	Servitude
Energy	⟷	Anxiety	Soft	⟷	Pushover
Fact	⟷	Story	Strength	⟷	Force
Good Enough	⟷	Perfect	Thermometer	⟷	Thermostat
Growth Mindset	⟷	Fixed Mindset	Transformation	⟷	Destruction
Impact	⟷	Intention	Vulnerability	⟷	Weakness
Influence	⟷	Power	Want	⟷	Need

Mindfulness & Somatic Wisdom

In this chapter we'll explore:

      A. Eating Raisins

      B. Inviting Your Somatic Wisdom

      C. The Art of Being, Not Doing

      D. Listening to Your Heart

      E. Absorbing the Beauty around You

      F. Multitasking Note to Self

      G. Meditation and Yoga

This chapter highlights a few of the many (many) practices you can do to strengthen the mind-body connection and listen to your internal wisdom. I actually have 54 of these practices that I selectively share with clients. I considered putting a whole bunch in here, simply because I love them all and different practices resonate differently with different people. But then I thought I might lose many of you if there were pages upon pages about it. So, I've selected my top seven. I have no idea why it's seven—it just is, though I could invent some story about it being tied to seven days of the week or something.

So here we have it. Perhaps, if you're a nonbeliever, you might be able to commit to trying out a couple in the coming week?

A. EATING RAISINS

Well, this may be one of the odder practices to try. But it's enlightening about our senses (all of them) and how we ignore most of them most of the time.

Go grab a box of raisins (or another nonfrozen treat).

I invite you to start by Grounding yourself (as described in Chapter 1) to become more present and aware.

We're going to start with the raisins still in the box, or your chosen treat. I'm quite certain not many of you selected carrot and celery sticks, but that's just my guess.

And we are going to SLOWLY notice the *box* of raisins with ALL five of our senses.

- What does the box *look* like?

- How does it *smell?*

- How does it *sound* when you shake it?

- How does it *feel* to the touch?

- How does it *taste?* (Yup, lick the box.)

Next, take a raisin out of the box and put it in your hand, repeating the same questions and observations.

Then put it in your mouth—but do not chew it yet—and ask the same questions.

Then chew it very (very) slowly. And finally, swallow it, all the while noticing your five senses. It's probably the longest you've ever taken to eat a raisin and might take as much as 10 minutes.

But I think you'll be surprised by what you notice when you focus your attention, presence, and energy on even a most familiar and common task like eating something. I'll leave you to draw your own conclusions from that.

B. INVITING YOUR SOMATIC WISDOM

Photo credit: Niloufar Nemati, Unsplash.com

Have you ever taken a self-induced time-out to listen to your body? Probably not. And why not? It is after all a fountain of knowledge that we perpetually ignore.

Consider taking two five-minute time-outs every day just to chill and listen to the wisdom contained within. I would suggest the first time could be when you awaken in bed, before your feet hit the ground (set your alarm five minutes early, if you must). The second time could be at a time that usually works well for you (say, before lunch or after dinner, or at noon every day, or at night while you brush those teeth, which of course I am sure we all do, every day, twice a day. Or not, but no one else knows it).

Sit or stand comfortably, with feet grounded below you, and arms gently on your lap or by your sides. Begin by taking five deep breaths. Then start to scan your body, from the top of your scalp, all the way down to your toes. Name the parts as you go and ask: "*How does this part feel today?*" Then relax it gently and move on to the next part.

When finished, if you are partial to journaling, take 30 seconds to jot down any insights or notes about what you felt or learned. For example, *I didn't know I held my tongue to the roof of my mouth* (you'd be surprised to hear how many clients report this). Or *Wow, my body is really tense and primed to fight the battle of the day.*

I am guessing there are many skeptics who might find these suggestions odd and skip to the next section. But just try it for a few days and see what you think. Many of my clients are pleasantly (or unpleasantly) surprised.

C. THE ART OF BEING, NOT DOING

"To-do" lists never stop. Ever. They serve a good purpose, but we can become a slave to them if we are not mindful. We are not wired to be running like a hamster on a wheel all the time! Discover the Art of Being, Not Doing. It's luxurious.

It starts with putting that to-do list aside, or better yet, renaming it a "Suggestions" list. After all, tomorrow is just a second chance to get done what was on today's to-do list. And most of it isn't life-threatening.

Start small. Block even 15 minutes a day to begin with. You might even venture into a whole morning or day. You can put this "being" on your to-do list if you must, but put it at the top. Use the time to just "be." Not to think about what to add to the to-do list, or what is next on the list, or what to fix, change, or perfect.

This time is important to our self-care (and sanity) and can be put to practice in many ways. For example:

- Sit quietly and meditate on how great you are and what you appreciate the most today.

- Go for a walk and explore what you see with an open mind and all senses. Note the beauty around you—it's surprising what you might discover (remember the eating-a-raisin exercise?)

- Use the time to do something you love that has no superficial "value."

- Bubble bath, anyone? Massage? Good book (and not a business one)?

- Secretly do something silly. When is the last time you jumped in a rain puddle? Have you sung in the shower much lately?

- Try something new. How about super-beginner nonjudgmental yoga in the privacy of your own home?

What's out there for *you*? Try this once a day, increasing your "do nothing" tolerance.

D. LISTENING TO YOUR HEART

Photo credit: Michelle Dot, Unsplash.com

Most of the time we are running ourselves ragged, getting the to-dos done and using our brains to do it. At other times, we focus on our bodies and get some good (and usually well-warranted) physical exercise. But what about our heart? Do we ever pause and nourish it? Probably not really.

Here's an interesting exercise to explore what your heart desires. Set aside 15 minutes for yourself in the evening (and before any sleep app chimes a reminder to go to bed). Put it in your calendar and be dogmatic about doing it for a couple of weeks.

Light a candle and put on some Spa Radio or Enya—or whatever soft music soothes you. Set a gentle 15-minute timer.

Sit in that comfy bedside chair with a warm blanket in the low-light glow of the candle. Breathe deeply. Do a five-minute body scan (see "B. Inviting Your Somatic Wisdom").

Then just sit quietly in meditation, asking your heart, "*What do I want for me going forward?*" Just keep coming back to that question.

Do not judge how your heart answers. Just let the thoughts be. Thank them and let them sit for a while or drift off if they don't resonate. Bring yourself back from any distracting thoughts like to-dos and let them float away. Just let them float by, like a soft cloud or a wisp of smoke—poof, and it is gone.

If you keep a journal, note any insights for later reflection.

E. ABSORBING THE BEAUTY AROUND YOU

Photo credit: Rose Arkadiy, Unsplash.com

Take a walk. Schedule it in your calendar, and just do it (as Nike would say).

Do NOT think about the day, the issues, the problems to solve. This is not about "clearing out" what is in your head or taking an inventory of your to-do list—rather, it's about "ingesting" the beauty and magic that surrounds you.

Go alone and in silence (no music, but headphones will help keep passersby at bay). Definitely do NOT take a dog, stroller, child, or friend.

Just notice what is around you. Look at the flowers; notice the faces of the people who pass you; listen for the birds, the trees rattling; smell the scent of freshly cut grass. Just look at what is out there and notice it. Don't analyze it, just let it be.

If your mind drifts, simply let the thoughts go, like clouds passing by and then going "poof!" like a wisp of smoke disappearing from a bonfire.

Notice how you feel (your head, your heart, your body). Notice anything cool you saw that you'd never noticed before. For example, have you ever stopped to notice how quickly spring flowers bloom over a week? It's pretty amazing. If you keep a journal, note any thoughts there. Consider doing this a couple of times a week to truly clear your mind and make room for focused thought at another time.

F. MULTITASKING NOTE TO SELF

Research by the Center for Brain Health (one of the leading authorities on these things) proves that chronic multitasking causes us to be:

- Constantly distracted

- Shallower thinkers

- Error prone

- Suckers for irrelevancy

- Rude and dismissive to those who crave our attention

And multitasking also leads to:

- Decline in fluid intelligence

- Greater brain atrophy

- Chronic stress

And yes, these findings are backed by the center's research and not just their speculations. Scary stuff.

Yet, as recently as a decade ago, over half of all résumés made reference to something about "being an excellent multitasker." How interesting is that? I don't think I've seen anyone sing the praises of multitasking recently. But that's not to say we don't continue to do it, constantly. Let's be honest, it happens all time.

A distinction I draw is between "multitasking" (say, chewing gum and walking at the same time, which sounds pretty safe to me) and "multi-focusing" (say, checking email while having a conversation with your partner). Clearly the latter is more problematic than the former.

So, if you haven't heard the message yet, or you're still a tad skeptical, I'd like to share a great demonstration you can try for yourself to illustrate just how poor we are in this regard.

For each of the three exercises below, set a timer for 30 seconds.

- *Trial 1:* Remember the childhood (or maybe still in your adulthood) game of "rock, paper, scissors"? Hope so. Take your left hand and roll through the "rock-paper-scissors" sequence as many times as you can without making a mistake. If you make a mistake, start over again. Note how many perfect sequences you can string together.

- *Trial 2:* This time, with your right hand, execute the following sequence: pat your tummy once, snap your fingers once; pat your tummy twice, snap your fingers twice; pat your tummy three times, snap your fingers three times. And so on. As in

Trial 1, start over if you make a mistake, and note how "high you can get a sequence in the 30 seconds.

- *Trial 3:* Now here's the proof. Conduct Trial 1 and Trial 2 at the same time.

I'll let you see for yourself just what horrible multitaskers we are, even for some pretty simple tasks. If you had the courage to take 90 seconds to try this set of exercises, I hope it remains as a vivid reminder for you!

And now, on to more productive thoughts and the seventh practice.

G. MEDITATION AND YOGA

Well, I just couldn't finish a chapter titled "Mindfulness & Somatic Wisdom" without putting in a good word for meditation and yoga. I just can't skip it, even though I am guessing that around half my readers are already passionate practitioners, and the other half are rampant avoiders. To each our own choices. I get it. Some of us don't want the hassle of scheduling a gym or studio visit, stifling in a hot room, sitting with a stiff back, or exposing ourselves to others' sweaty breath. Never mind how ridiculous we might appear in a downward dog or attempting to balance on one leg.

But I have an idea for you to consider. For those anti-yogis, I invite you to check out one (free) app called FitOn. It allows you to set parameters that suit you and your schedule, including level of difficulty and length of time. Personally, I set it at difficulty of 1 and maximum of 10 minutes—and then, if I'm feeling motivated, I can just do two routines back to back. It even has 2-minute "work workouts" focused on stretches that can be done at your office desk. I mean really, how convenient is that?

Anyway, enough preaching about it. If you have any secret inkling to give it a try in the privacy of your home, here's what the app looks like (it's purple):

For those of you who are possibly anti-meditators, I offer you these stats. With practiced meditation,

- 76% reported better general wellness

- 60% felt they had more energy

- 50% noticed sharper memory and focus

- 29% reduced their anxiety

- 22% reduced their stress

- 18% reduced their depression

Sounds pretty good, right? So, if you even have 10–20 minutes a day to check it out (especially before bed), here are some apps that my clients and I have found to be easy, fun, and helpful:

Choosing Narratives

Everyone has a "Current Narrative"—the way we *are* in our current environment, what we're *experiencing*, and how we're *being*.

These narratives vary all over the board. The most common Current Narratives I hear from women returning from maternity leave are:

- *"The Hamster on a Treadmill."* She just keeps going and going on the treadmill of life, exhausting herself while going the distance, day after day after day.

- *"The Rubik's Cube."* She is trying to figure out how all the pieces fit together and can be organized; she's constantly putting the puzzle together.

- *"Superwoman."* She is attempting to do all things, for all people, with great time pressure and expectations. Superpowers on the outside.

Photo credit: Miguel Bruna, Unsplash.com

- *"The Tightrope Walker."* She aspires to stay on top of things and not fall off her precarious balance.

Photo credit: Aleksandr Kadykov, Unsplash.com

- *"The Juggler."* She challenges herself to keep all the balls in the air and not let one drop.

Photo credit: Alexey Turenkov, Unsplash.com

- *"The Guarded Heart under Attack."* She feels trapped and attacked from all angles, looking for a route to escape and waiting for the next lightning bolt to hit.

Do any of these resonate with you? Do you have an image with some words that sum up your life? Pause and think about it—name it, picture it. Check out www.Unsplash.com for some free images to download for inspiration.

Not exactly a pretty picture for those who have gone blindly into this major life transition! Of course, may new moms have much more appealing Current Narratives. But these themes are surprisingly common by the time I meet with my clients. You may not identify with any of the above narratives and may be able to describe your own Current Narrative if you dig deep. But one thing's for sure—whatever your narrative is, it's only going to intensify, if it hasn't already.

In writing this book, my hope for you is that you can migrate toward a deeper narrative. One in which you are more calm, balanced, focused, wise, and sage. This picture captures it for me. I call it *"The Wise Grounded Woman."*

Source: New Ventures West

Taking Stock

In this chapter we'll explore:

    A. Your Legacy

    B. Knowing Your Priorities

    C. Urgent/Important Matrix

    D. Performance/Potential Matrix

    E. Message from Your Older, Wiser Self

A. YOUR LEGACY

What do you want to be remembered for?

Stepping back to the longest-term perspective, many refer to the "Gravestone" exercise or the "Obituary" exercise or the "Funeral Commentary" exercise. All these (somewhat morbid) exercises look at the values you held, the principles you lived by, and how you made

Photo credit:
John Thomas, Unsplash.com

others feel. It can be a list of key words, or a simple statement ("*She was an incredible mother and wife*").

If you haven't thought about it already, a good starting point is to consider what you want to be remembered for. Very few people identify the kinds of things that would go on such a list. It's often things at a much higher and enduring level, things that can even be quite spiritual or cosmic in nature.

Here's a spot for you to jot down your thoughts.

____

____

____

____

____

If you're stuck, here's something called the "Legacy Exercise" that might offer some inspiration. Often, when we think about our legacy, we think in grandiose terms like "generations to come" and "eternity."

Well, guess what? Your direct "legacy" is likely to span only a couple of generations. That realization helps us pull in our thinking somewhat.

To illustrate:

1. Think of your two parents. What were their names? What did they do?

   Mom: ______________________________________

   Dad: ______________________________________

   (Of course, this exercise becomes even more complex if you feel you have more than two "parents." In that case, add them here too.)

2. Think of your four grandparents. What were their names? What did they do?

   Maternal Grandma: _______________________________

   Maternal Grandad: _______________________________

   Paternal Grandma: _______________________________

   Paternal Grandad:_______________________________

3. Think of your eight great-grandparents. What were their names? What did they do?

   Maternal Grandma's Mom:_______________________________

   Maternal Grandma's Dad:_______________________________

   Maternal Grandad's Mom: _______________________________

   Maternal Grandad's Dad: _______________________________

   Paternal Grandma's Mom: _______________________________

   Paternal Grandma's Dad: _______________________________

   Paternal Grandad's Mom: _______________________________

   Paternal Grandad's Dad: _______________________________

4. Think of your 16 great-great-grandparents. What were their names? What did they do?

   Maternal Grandma's Mom's Mom: _______________________________

   Maternal Grandma's Mom's Dad: _______________________________

   Maternal Grandma's Dad's Mom: _______________________________

   Maternal Grandma's Dad's Dad: _______________________________

Maternal Grandad's Mom's Mom:_______________________

Maternal Grandad's Mom's Dad:_______________________

Maternal Grandad's Dad's Mom: _______________________

Maternal Grandad's Dad's Dad: _______________________

Paternal Grandma's Mom's Mom: _______________________

Paternal Grandma's Mom's Dad:_______________________

Paternal Grandma's Dad's Mom:_______________________

Paternal Grandma's Dad's Dad:_______________________

Paternal Grandad's Mom's Mom: _______________________

Paternal Grandad's Mom's Dad: _______________________

Paternal Grandad's Dad's Mom: _______________________

Paternal Grandad's Dad's Dad: _______________________

OK, now my head is spinning with all the combinations. And, at least for me, the "fill in the lines" are mostly blank, even if just trying to recall their names.

I won't even challenge you to list the names and occupations of your 32 great-great-great grandparents, because unless you're heavily into ancestry and genealogy, you'll fall into the 99 percent of the population who can name none, or only one, or maybe two.

My point here being that we typically can't even remember our ancestors' names. Let alone their occupations or what they were all about. We might recall an anecdotal tale or vivid story that has been passed down through the generations. Maybe even a broader set of "family values" or "family mottos"—though these are rarely attributable to a particular individual. So, the identifiable lasting impact you'll have is really only on the next couple of generations. Does that help you narrow down the scope of what you want to be remembered for?

Let's go back to the list you drafted at the beginning of this chapter and revise and build on it. Here's a fresh space to note down your updated draft of what you want to be remembered for. (This may well be further refined as you continue to ponder it.)

____

____

____

____

____

B. KNOWING YOUR PRIORITIES

OK, with that "Legacy List" drafted, I'm guessing you will find it quite conceptual, aspirational, and lofty. Then, in many respects, it's challenging to figure out quite what to do with it today. So what? What does it mean? What do you do with that? What does it imply for your personal priorities today? Figuring out priorities is actually more challenging than you might initially think, right?

Let's start at the conceptual level. What are the big-picture items that matter most to you? The list might include a handful or two. For example:

- Personal fulfillment
- Family security

- Depth of friendships

- Exploring the world

- Contributing to community

- Improving the world

- Serving the underprivileged

- Growing a strong partnership

- Adventuring in life

- Becoming an expert on something unique

- Teaching others how to learn

- Conquering mountains

- Bettering the environment

- Being the best possible parent

- Achieving career greatness

The list of possibilities goes on and on. It's personal. And for most, it's hard to do.

Take a few minutes to think about it and jot down your top 10 thoughts as they come to you in a stream of consciousness. Now put it away for a couple of days and mark this page in your book, to revisit later.

Your incoming Priorities list:

____

____

____

____

____

____

____

Come back to it and reflect, modify, add, and delete. Iterate on this in the coming weeks until you have something that feels right. Not perfect, just close.

C. URGENT/IMPORTANT MATRIX

So, now that you are clear on your Legacy aspirations and your Priorities, let's take a look at how you're applying them.

How are you spending your time? Here's an interesting framework: the "Urgent/Important" matrix.

- *Urgent*: Things that really do need to be done now. The pressing issues. Things that you may have put off until they became urgent. The time-sensitive stuff.

- *Important*: Things that align most tightly with your Legacy aspirations and Priorities. What actually matters in the scheme of things (for whatever reason).

The four-quadrant matrix that emerges can be pretty telling. Consider for a moment where you are spending most of your time. Remember the Rocks-Pebbles-Sand concept from Chapter 1? Think about where yours lie on the matrix. In concept, the "rocks" fall on the right-hand side, the "sand" tends to lie on the left, and the pebbles are scattered throughout.

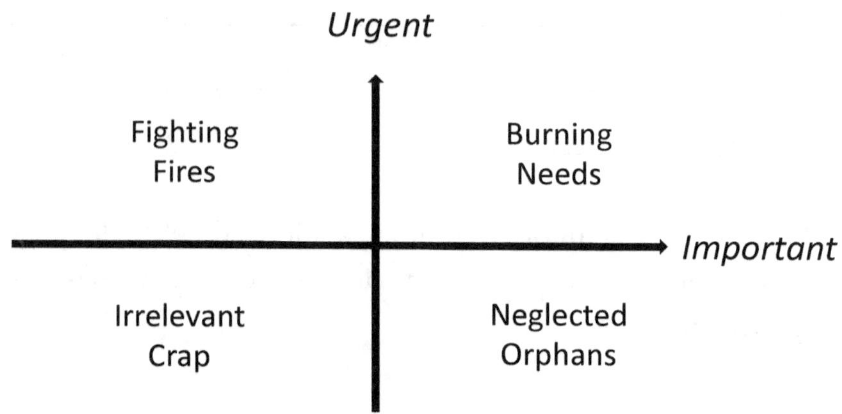

See if you can fill in the matrix with where you have been spending your time. If you're stuck, take a look at your to-do list, explicit or implicit. Or look at your calendar for the last few months. Here's a blank matrix for you to contemplate on.

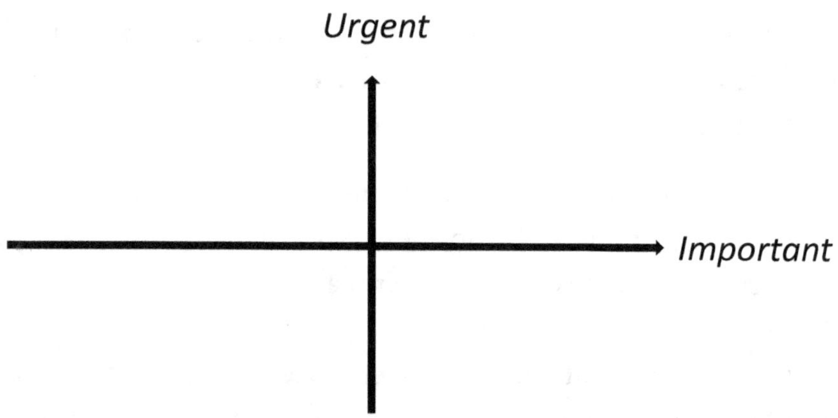

Some clients have chosen to keep a whiteboard of their urgent-important matrix, rather than a linear list (e.g., the dreaded to-do list). A whiteboard keeps it fluid and helps put things in perspective. It also allows change on the fly—and wiping items off (as we have been accustomed to doing with that dreaded to-do list).

Finally, if you find this framework intriguing, here's how to take it up another level. Consider giving weight to how big some of these activities are. How much effort do they take? You can draw bigger circles for the items that take a lot of time and smaller circles for those that take less. It's conceptual. But it's rather enlightening. Many find that their:

- *Lower left (Irrelevant Crap)* quadrant of the matrix is where a bunch of the "sand" lies and takes up an inordinate amount of collective time.

- *Upper left (Fighting Fires)* takes up the majority of their time and causes a lot of anxiety and time pressure.

- *Upper right (Burning Needs)* is pretty big and heavily weighted.

- *Lower right (Neglected Orphans)* is pretty sparse, in reality. (As a side note, reading this book likely falls into this quadrant. So, kudos to you for exploring this far. And for making the time to focus on something that's important but never urgent).

URGENT/IMPORTANT MATRIX ... WEIGHTED BY EFFORT

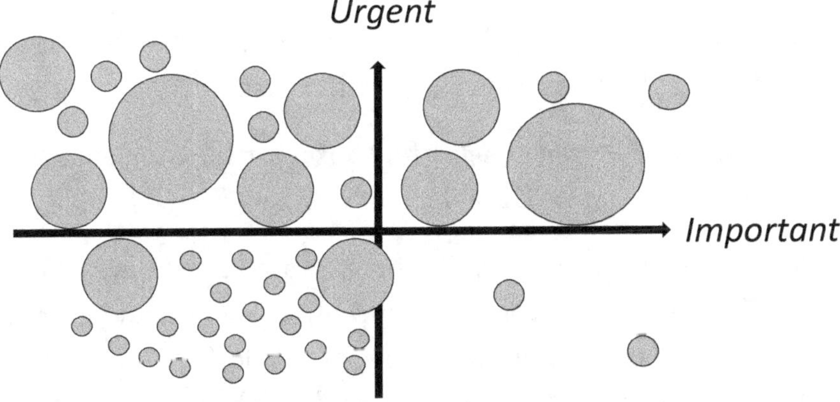

Happy pondering and exploring!

D. PERFORMANCE/POTENTIAL MATRIX

Many companies use a "Performance/Potential" matrix to evaluate the career development of their leadership pipeline. Often it is called the "nine box." If you're not familiar with it, here's how it is laid out.

PERFORMANCE/POTENTIAL MATRIX

Performance:			
Strong			
Acceptable			
Poor			
Potential:	Low	Medium	High

You can layer in color coding (red-orange-yellow-green) to make it visual, or use black and white (from dark to light). In general:

- People falling into the *red (black)* box find themselves on an exit plan.

- Those in the *orange (dark gray)* boxes find themselves on some form of PIP (Performance Incentive Plan).

- Those in the *yellow (light gray)* boxes are likely on some form of PDP (Personal Development Plan).

- And those in the *green (white)* box are very well positioned. They get the big bonus and incentive payouts, and everyone pays a lot of attention to how to develop and retain them. These are often known as "HiPos" (High Performance/High Potential).

- Most of us who reach leadership positions have a good track record of both performance and potential (white or light gray: somewhere in the three boxes of the upper-right corner.

PERFORMANCE/POTENTIAL MATRIX

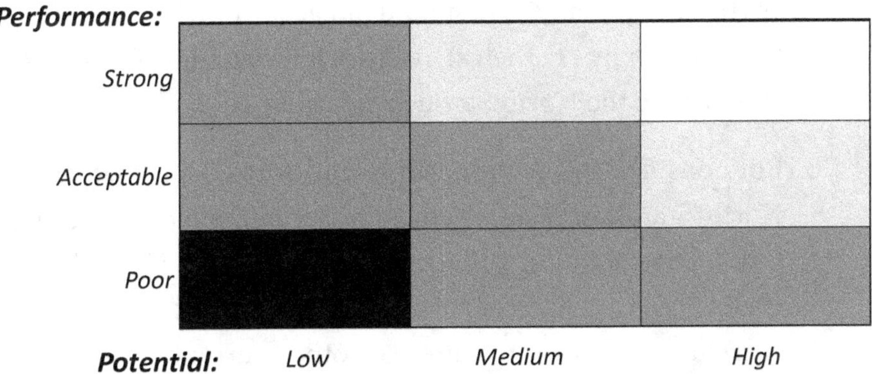

You are likely familiar with this thinking from a career perspective, either conceptually or in practice at review time. I have three important challenges for you to consider regarding the Performance/Potential (nine-box) framework.

1. Have you thought about this for yourself, outside of the work context? At work, we typically get annual or semiannual performance reviews, including some form of assessment on performance-potential. Yet, as the "CEO of you," have you ever taken stock of how you're doing on your nonwork priorities (your life!)? How are you doing in other areas of your life (as a partner, a friend, a daughter)? It might be worth some consideration. It can be quite enlightening to place your key priorities or roles on the matrix above.

2. Most aspiring leaders expect to be in the upper-right (white) box. And we can become pretty unmotivated if we are not— arguing about it, becoming upset about it. Which I believe

has often led to companies refining and expanding the green box even further: to "high" and "very high" and even "exceptional" segments. A disproportionate percentage of the leadership population often simply get classified into the upper-right (white) box. Many green-box leaders, not wanting to be anything less than the best (and not accustomed to being anything less than #1) then strive to achieve the illusive topmost spot, where the North Star lies.

3. But consider this: Getting into, and staying in, that elusive North Star box takes an inordinate amount of dedication, focus, time, and energy. And you cannot be a North Star in everything you do. So, consider asking yourself whether your current career, in the context of other current or imminent priorities, is something you really want to aspire to being at the top of? This is likely a foreign concept for many readers. Just think for now about whether being "very good" is better than "outstandingly, untouchable, exceptional" in the relative scheme of things. It's not that you wouldn't be able to reprioritize at a future moment in time, as life's journey unfolds.

PERFORMANCE/POTENTIAL MATRIX

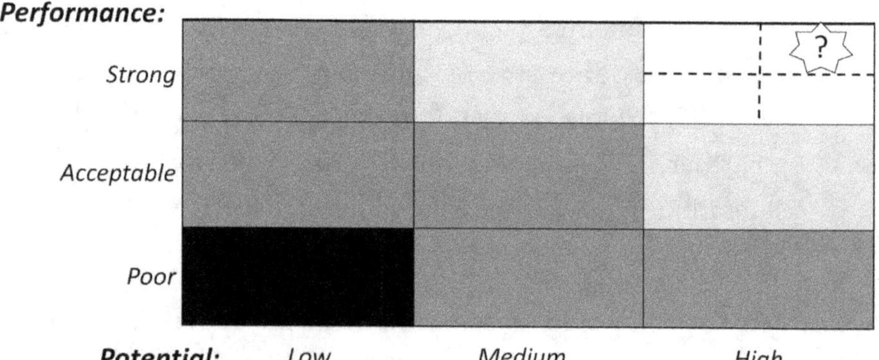

E. MESSAGE FROM YOUR OLDER, WISER SELF

Well, if you've waded through this chapter on taking stock of yourself, and have taken the time to absorb, explore, and consider, you may not be in the mood for what follows (in which case, skip to the next chapter). But you may be up for this final section, which can really add the icing to the cake. This exercise provides yet another lens of insight into where you are at this point in your journey.

Here's how it goes:

1. Start by Grounding yourself (see Chapter 1).

2. With your eyes closed, go "inside" yourself, observing your being as you are today. Notice the smallest, most discrete functions of your body. How is your heart beating? How does your tummy feel? What is going on inside your very being? Get really granular and really small.

3. Then, pull yourself "up" and out of your body. Observe yourself and your body. Then your environment. Then your place on this earth. Then your dot on the earth from far above. Look at yourself from a much higher vantage point. Look down on yourself as a speck in the universe.

4. Now, pause and ask yourself:

   a. *"What's important for me to pay attention to?"*
   b. *"What's not important that I shouldn't worry about?"*
   c. *"What advice do I have about how to live my life?"*

5. After reflecting and absorbing what your higher, sage self has to say, slowly descend from the meta-view to the micro-view. Take your time, descend back into your body slowly and thoughtfully.

6. Take three deep cleansing breaths, and when you are ready, open your eyes and come back to reality.

7. Note down any advice that came to mind.

Source: The New York Public Library, Unsplash.com

I realize this exercise is a bit woo-woo for some. But if they have the curiosity to experiment with it, many clients share that it is a truly revealing experience that you can have from the comfort of your own home, without expectations, and in less than 15 minutes. I throw it out there for your playful self to experiment with!

You Can't Control the World

As I mentioned earlier, we cannot change the past, nor can we predict the future (remember FEAR from Chapter 6?). And we cannot control the world and everything around us. Yet so many of us allow our egos to take hold and believe we can. This forcing of control is exhausting. Sometimes we just need to let go and let things evolve and unfold. The graphic below highlights some of the things that are in and out of our control.

WHAT'S IN MY CONTROL? THE GRAY CIRCLE!

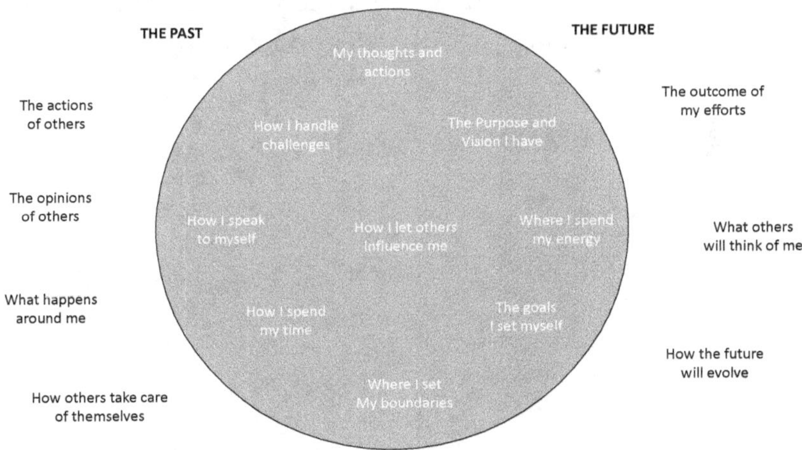

So, what does this have to do with the arrival of a baby? A lot!

We women leaders, thriving in fast-paced environments, often tend to be:

- Perfectionists

- Planners

- Control freaks

- Doers

- Driven

- Confident

- Secure

- Reliable

And well, babies quite simply are not any of these things. They can throw us off-kilter and into an unknown realm of chaos. They can drive us crazy, causing a lot of angst and insecurity.

My advice to you is to recognize and accept that you will no longer be "in control"—and that is perfectly fine. Let go and enjoy the ride—you'll eventually end up at the same destination! Just that one journey's path is far more enjoyable than the other.

UNDERSTAND YOUR CURRENT EMPLOYMENT SITUATION

Part One may well seem like a rather lengthy prelude about "knowing thyself" to what you likely picked up this book for—to help guide you down the journey of pausing and reentering work along the magic of the maternity path.

I really do embrace (and hope you see) the importance of exploring you first—what YOU really want, where you come from, the life stage you are in, the natural state of your being, the importance of mindset, the critical value of mindfulness and somatic wisdom, choosing narratives, taking stock, and the reality that you can't control the world.

It's a lot to absorb, and if you've been powering through this book, may I suggest that you take a deep breath, pause, and just *be* for a moment? Or a day. Or a week. Unless your due date is imminent.

This journey is not a race, and sometimes thoughtful breaks go a long way to giving ourselves space for reflection and absorption.

So now, as my dad used to say before starting a bedtime story, *"Are you sitting comfortably? Then we shall begin"* (with Part Two).

To Work or Not to Work—
That Is the Question

As I started out to write this book I asked myself, "Who am I really speaking to?" And "Who is my target audience?" (As all good businesspeople, and marketers in particular, do: Thank you, Procter & Gamble training of decades ago.) My conclusion is that I hope to reach women who *think* they want to return to work with their current employer. But so much is a gray area, from whether to return at all to whether to return to the employment situation you are taking a leave from. No one (ever) knows everything for sure. As I've mentioned before, we can't predict the future, nor should we fear it.

If you are absolutely certain that you never want to resume a career outside the home, then please do put this book down, go take a relaxing bubble bath (you'll need it when embarking on the all-important and challenging journey of working within the home), and come back to it when or if your thinking changes. If you are still planning or even considering a return, then carry on!

The question of whether or not to work outside the home is a deeply (deeply!) personal one. Let me be clear, there is no "right" answer. Only the one that works best for you, at least for right now. It can migrate and even change over time.

In my experience, I went (on delivery day minus one) from

- *"Absolutely, of course I'm a career-oriented woman who could never be a stay-at-home mom"* ("*Skipped 3 grades of school! Harvard MBA with Distinction! Fast-track BCGer!*")

- To (actual day of delivery) *"Hell no, I could never leave this precious baby girl to the care of anyone else. Are you crazy?!"*

- To *"OMG, I am going insane singing 'itsy bitsy spider' and I need to get back to finding me—and something where my mind is more challenged."*

Like I said, it's a journey and there are no perfect answers. My journey certainly took its twists and turns.

- **First maternity leave.** Charlotte was born five weeks early, and I was one month shy of my much-anticipated promotion from Consultant to Project Leader (23 of 24 months' tenure didn't cut it, apparently! I was rather annoyed about that part). I had initially planned on three months off, an office transfer from London to Boston, and a return-to-work full time. Roll on to the actual arrival, and I decided I could never leave my precious baby girl to a stranger. Decided to quit. Met with one of BCG's first employee hires, and then head of the New York Office—Sandy Moose (amazing woman, btw). She persuaded me to come back 25% (one day in the office, plus a little extra) working on some internal knowledge development. Then she enticed me with interesting upcoming client work, with add-on comments like *"Oh, but that's right, you only want to do a day a week of internal work, so forget I mentioned that."* Brilliant! Roll on a month or so, and I couldn't resist a cool new piece of client work, and "poof!" I was back to 50%, which turned out to be a little underweighted, with commitments to recruiting and other internal roles. (I was, at the time, one of the few examples of "working moms" to trot out in front of potential new hires.) So, 60% was invented. And it worked well.

- **Second maternity leave.** About two years later, in the freezing New York/Connecticut winter, my son Matthew was born. With a delivery in February, and a three-month leave, that put my technical return to work in May. Um, but that was the start of summer! And my parents had an amazing cottage in Canada, and well, I just wanted to hang out on the lake with the family. So, I extended leave by another (unpaid) four months and returned to work in the fall. Initially it was 60%. But then fun and interesting work came up, so it went to 80%. Then that was too much, so I went to 70% (three days in the office, plus some wiggle room for other activities like recruiting). But then a super-cool opportunity came up and I went back full time. Plus, I wanted that upcoming promotion! I was lucky, I had a super nanny situation, and everything was stable. For a bit.

- **Third maternity leave.** Building up to this one was a burnout challenge. At the time, my husband was in the crazy internet-start-up days of the early 2000s, and so was spending much of his time in Austin, Texas, while I was juggling a 5-year-old, a 2.5-year-old (ugh—those toddler years!!!), and a third-trimester pregnancy. All while living in Stamford, Connecticut, commuting an hour to our Manhattan office— and oh, with a client in Los Angeles. It was a nightmare of work stress, but I held out and hung in there. And I got that much coveted promotion. Sarah was born in May, and the kids and I joined my children's father in Austin a week before the on-time delivery—exactly five years and a day after my first baby was born. (I stayed very still on Sarah's due date, since it happened to be Charlotte's 5th birthday and I didn't want them to have to share that special day.) After the trauma of the previous six months, I decided to quit. For sure! After all, we were then in Austin, chasing wild and crazy emerging internet dreams! But BCG said, "*Just keep the laptop for now.*" And I did. And then the internet bubble burst. So, we spent much of the next four months traveling and escaping reality, with three children under 5 in tow. It was FUN. But then someone needed to pay the mortgage on the market-crashing, devaluating home. So, I went reluctantly back to work. (We flipped a coin to decide whether my then-husband or I would go back to work, and I lost.) Since BCG didn't have an Austin office back then, we moved to Dallas, where I could avoid the always-being-cancelled late-night final-leg flight segment to Austin. From that point on, I was largely full time, and my children's father was the more at-home parent in those early years.

My point in sharing my journey is simply that everyone's journey unfolds in different and unexpected ways. It's a bit like surfing a wave—you gotta go with the flow and be agile. To do what's best for you and your family in the moment. And you don't have to decide for sure how you're going to spend your entire parenting career. Since you're reading this book, you are likely a high-achieving leader, and options for work will always be out there. Just go with what works for you in the now, as the situation reveals itself.

Let's get back to the root of the question. "*Shall I work or not work?*" can seem daunting and permanent. But it doesn't have to be. Let's reframe it:

- It's not "all or none" or "yes or no"—there are varieties and nuances that best suit you.

- It's what works for you now—it's not a long-term forever decision.

- You can always change your mind!

I am going to assume that if you're still reading this book, you are leaning toward (or at least considering) returning to work outside the home—in some way, shape, or fashion.

With that in mind, a good starting point is to really understand where you are in your career (the "reality check"), what your current employer offers, and where the intersection of those two lies. Within the intersection there are many options to explore, often including part time, flextime, and shared/split time.

If your intersection is empty, then, it's time to look for a more enlightened employer who might co-create options in that intersection of "you and them."

You: Reality Check

In this chapter we'll explore:

    A. Current Role

    B. Trajectory

    C. Time-Warp Scenario Game

A. CURRENT ROLE

Start by considering where you are at work *today*.

- What role are you in?

- What do you like about it?

- What do you not like about it?

- What would you keep doing/stop doing/change about it if you could?

- Overall, are you happy in it? What does it do for you? Why are you in it?

Write it down. If you just think about it in concept, you'll likely not really delve into the present. Take a moment to jot down the answers to the questions above here.

____

____

____

____

____

____

____

____

B. TRAJECTORY

Take a super-high-level look at your career track to date. Draw a horizontal line (for a timeline) on the page, with "first big-girl job" at the left and the line extending out for, say, the following 10 years. Note where you are today on the timeline, and where key promotions and changes have happened. Then look ahead a few years on what you aspire to. Do you see key promotions? Important career shifts? Key milestones?

Get a sense of where you've been, where you are, and where you are going. It doesn't have to be perfect. The aim is to be generally correct (though you know it will be specifically wrong!).

You might even overlay other key events in your nonwork life. For example, is there another baby on the horizon sometime in the next few years? (Gasp, do I even suggest this to a third-trimester reader?!)

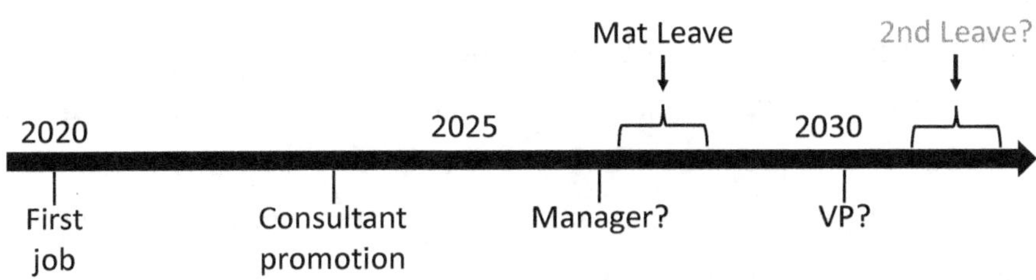

Now it's your turn to create one for yourself.

YOUR 10-YEAR TIMELINE

C. TIME-WARP SCENARIO GAME

You've probably written your timeline trajectory as though it was "business (or life) as usual" and working in your current capacity, which is likely "100%" right now.

Now it's time to play the career-planning (or time-warp) scenario game.

Consider for a moment the implications of what happens if you take extended leaves. What about if you go part time for extended periods? What about another maternity leave somewhere on the horizon? At this point it can start to get complicated, with timelines shifting and assumptions flying.

Some of my clients have used an Excel spreadsheet (admittedly, the highly analytical ones, and certain Enneagram types in particular). The basic concept is to create a spreadsheet that goes month-by-month or quarter-by-quarter—with the time block, the capacity in which you might work in that time frame, and the implications on career-path (and promotion) timing.

It simply puts in black and white the implications of decisions on path-forward. There's no right or wrong; it's simply an exercise in understanding options. For example, if a promotion is 12 months out, and you decide to go 50% capacity at work, that promotion now becomes 24 months out. And if you are considering another maternity leave in a couple of years, that promotion becomes 30 months out with a 6-month parental leave. And so on.

Create one for yourself if you are perusing some key work-capacity options.

You: Your Brand

In this chapter we'll explore:

    A. An Honest Look at Feedback

    B. Wordle

    C. Johari Window

A. AN HONEST LOOK AT FEEDBACK

The dreaded F-word. No, not that one! Feedback.

Unless you are the most amazing, sky-rocketing superstar, those annual or semiannual performance reviews likely contain some stinging comments and piss-me-off suggestions. We high achievers are not generally pleased about hearing "opportunities for improvement." Yet there are some real nuggets in there. And if they are thoughtfully and authentically described, there's a lot to learn from it. Even if we don't like it.

So, pull out those reviews of the last few years. Reread them, without getting judgmental about yourself or the author. Just take them for what they're worth and assume good intent. Highlight the comments that are insightful—the good and the bad.

Now step back and write your own career performance review. Just for you. Consider answering the following three questions:

1. What am I really strong at? Great at? What helps me excel?

2. What truly are my "areas for development"? What could use some work? Where is my growth-edge?

3. What do I need to do to get from here to there? What will support my growth? Where are my resources?

B. WORDLE

Now that we've finished that (humbling) experience of looking ourselves in the mirror regarding career feedback, let's move on to something more fun!

Have you ever heard of a wordle? It's where you create a list of words, assign them weighted importance, and get a graphical output of how that looks—a word "cloud." They are often used in concept development, visioning, and branding.

Consider what your brand wordle might look like, and create one now. A free site I appreciate is www.EdWordle.net. Set aside 30 minutes to start, create a list of the words you want your career brand to stand for, and get started in seeing what the output looks like. This is fun to noodle on.

Please note, though, that as you revise your inputs, each graphic you create is unique and will be replaced when you push the return key again. So, if you find one that is pretty good and you might want to keep it, be sure to screenshot it. You might not like the updated graphic as much as the previous one.

I really hope you do this, because it's a lot of creative fun. You might not get to the perfect wordle on the first go-round, but you can always come back and play with it. Some of my clients keep it in their top desk drawer as their own personal North Star that they aspire to. A couple of clients even framed it and hang it (discreetly) on their wall.

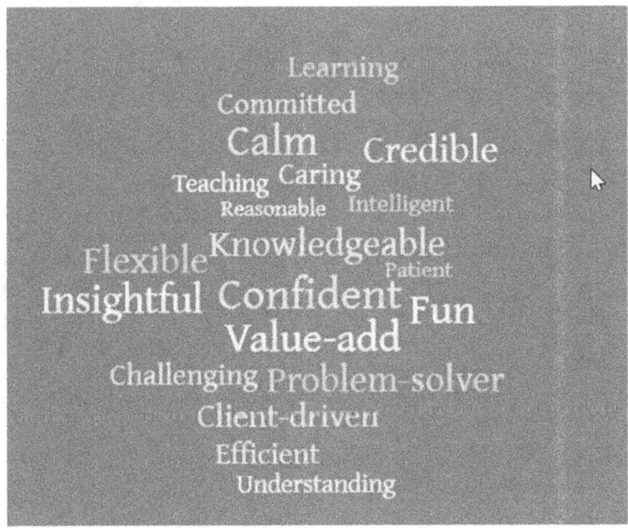

What words belong in yours? Start with a random string of thoughts—then start *wordling* it.

____

____

____

____

____

C. JOHARI WINDOW

The Johari Window may be a bit of a sidebar here, but I think it's worth mentioning. Now that you've clearly identified what your own "Brand You" is, the Johari Window framework takes a look at how visible your brand is to you and to others.

- *Open:* In the upper left is what you know about you, and what others know about you. It is the you that comes to top of mind.

- *Blind:* In the upper right is what others know of or see in you, but that you might not be naturally aware of. On the encouraging side, these can be the kinds of things about which you say, *"Oh wow, that's great to hear—I didn't realize that!"*

- *Facade:* In the lower left is what you truly know about yourself, but others simply don't see. They are the hidden gems, the things you wish people knew about the real you: the opportunities you have to make your authentic self more visible.

- *Unknown:* In the lower right is what no one sees—you or others—that might be hidden beneath the tip of the iceberg.

It's uncharted, undiscovered territory that might reveal itself as your journey unfolds. It can often be driven by the Clifton Strengths (discussed in Chapter 5) that lurk beneath the surface.

JOHARI WINDOW FRAMEWORK

	To Self	
	Known	Unknown
To Others		
Known	OPEN	BLIND
Unknown	FACADE	UNKNOWN

After you have thought about "Brand You," pausing to consider your Johari Window can often reveal some interesting insights. You might even consider asking trusted others what they see. Their input may well surprise you!

YOUR JOHARI WINDOW

	To Self	
	Known	Unknown
To Others		
Known		
Unknown		

Them: Your Current Employer

In this chapter we'll explore:

> A. Opportunities Employers Present
>
> B. Benefits and Policies They Provide

A. OPPORTUNITIES EMPLOYERS PRESENT

Let's start with the fundamentals here.

What does your current employment provide YOU? Why are you choosing to work there?!

Sometimes we forget to clearly articulate these things as we plod along our career, development, and compensation paths.

The vast majority of my clients are in that elusive 10% who actually work not just because they *have* to but because they *love* to. Some of us are fortunate to be people whose jobs (on most days) bring us joy. For them, work is not "work."

So, why do you get up in the morning and go to (or Zoom to) work? What is it that motivates you (and I don't just mean the money side of things)? What do you LOVE about your work? What gets you excited? Why do you do it? What's your inspiration?

Pause for a moment and jot down your reflections on the questions above about what your employer provides *you*:

____

____

____

____

____

B. BENEFITS AND POLICIES THEY PROVIDE

Putting aside the mega picture of what leave opportunities your employer provides and how you value which components of them, let's shift gears to the specifics of what you can expect from your employer in that short period of time—The Leave.

Pull out that dusty "employee handbook." Or better yet, get the most up-to-date intranet policies about leaves and know what they say. In writing. There are often a handful of components:

- *Length of basic maternity leave.* How long you can disappear for. It varies hugely by geography. Whereas US-based companies tend to provide only 3 months, European companies often provide as long as 12 months. And Canadian companies tend to offer as many as 18 months (with some caveats).

- *Extension of leave.* There are often additional specifications about adding vacation days to the time period, or taking unpaid leaves of absence (sometimes only if bookended with the maternity leave itself).

- *Compensation.* Typically, it is full base compensation, with widely varying expectations on bonus and incentive compensation (if at all applicable during the time of the leave).

- *Health care benefits.* All health care policies will cover pre-natal, delivery, and postpartum care. Some may have caveats about preexisting condition and length of employment. All will require the enrollment of your new bundle of joy into the family policy. Some have very generous benefits. (One of my clients calls their employer's policy the "$5 baby policy" because the only out-of-pocket expense is the initial maternity visit copay.) Others have more complex processes and approvals, and widely varying out-of-pocket expense implications depending on how closely you follow them.

These basics are usually quite succinctly summarized, and generally have little wiggle room from the black-and-white policy in ink. Consider these policies to be the "table stakes." They are not generally (re-)negotiable. As we'll explore shortly, though, you need to consider a number of nuances and additional flexibility about how you handle the specifics of your leave and return.

Give Yourself Grace

Photo credit: Amanda Vickers, Unsplash.com

Before we delve into this part about exploring, planning, and taking action, I thought it worth a moment to pause and remind yourself about the drive to "get it all done" before leave starts. Let's be realistic—it could start anytime, and you would survive (and thrive) without having completed your to-do list.

Consider taking a break. Like right now. How about a nap? A bubble bath? One of those pregnancy massages? This book can wait until you're done just "being" and not "doing."

Pregnancy, as you well know, comes with limitations—not just the obvious physical ones, but also the emotional, relational, mental, and spiritual ones. It's a lot, and it's tempting to just work through them. But now is a great time to dial back a little and consider some alternate approaches:

- Stop trying to do it all.

- Make "slow down" your motto.

- Let go of absolutes—there's usually a gray area.

- Learn to set boundaries.

- Look for compromises.

- Lean on dear friends and colleagues and off-load tasks (they usually truly want to help!).

- Practice saying no—it is, indeed, a complete sentence.

There is an art and a science to just "being" and not constantly "doing." It's OK, no one is going to grade you on the completion of your to-do list!

Scrutinize Your HR Policy, Then Think Beyond

Photo credit: Tim Gouw, Unsplash.com

The official and formal policies run the gamut of programs. And no doubt by now you've already checked out the official policies (either at the first sign of a double line; if not, well before or since then). And you've probably also had a conversation with HR. That's the obvious and the formal. It typically covers the official days/weeks of paid leave offered, options for extended (unpaid) leaves, how vacation days are to be handled, how bonuses are handled, and the benefits (health care) provided for prenatal care and delivery.

Then there are the unofficial wiggle-room conversations. What if you want to start leave before the due date? What if you are forced to start leave due to an early delivery? What if you do a couple of days work during leave? What if the email doesn't stop piling in? Who's going to cover for you? How should you word your out-of-office? What should you do if a client or customer calls? How are you going to share revenues and client credits?

The permutations and possible conversations are endless. If there are some that keep you up at night, raise them. If there are others you simply ponder, then just relax, don't worry about it. A good employee-employer relationship will figure out the off-radar topics if and when they arise. No one is going to die if you did (or did not) get paid for an hour's work or a day's sick leave. Sometimes we can obsess way (way) more than is necessary.

Ask around to understand what others have done, and where challenges arose. Learn from the mistakes of others.

But then, "go with the flow" and "ride the wave." Ask for forgiveness, not permission. There are a ton of adages offering advice. It's all good, and life as we know it will go on.

Reconsider Shutting Down the Laptop

Photo credit: James McKinven, Unsplash.com

Conventional (and politically correct) wisdom screams, "*shut down your laptop*" and "*take full advantage of your leave benefit.*" Good advice, especially in the short term. I'm not arguing against those philosophies at all. But I am going to challenge you to think through the wisdom of heeding that advice 100%.

First off, is it realistic to shut down the laptop and dust it off in a couple of months? What about Slack, Chat, WhatsApp, Teams, LinkedIn, Zoom, voicemail, and whatever else you habitually use? Let's be honest, I've yet to meet a woman who really, truly "shut everything off" except her personal Gmail. So, there's the reality factor, which you'll want to consider how you'll handle.

Also, there's the practicality and wisdom of going AWOL for months at a time. Granted, some of you have jobs from which you can walk away for an extended period and simply pick back up on return. All the power to you!

But most of us have careers where continuity and relationships are important, particularly in the professional services (consulting, financial advising, advertising, legal, etc.). In these fields, relationships tend to be longer-term, partnerships build from a slow boil, and needs, requests, and proposals often have longer runways than, say, day-to-day operations. Add to that well-intentioned colleagues who may step in temporarily but have a difficult time letting go and handing it back to you upon your return.

As always, there's no right answer here. Yet it's worth getting clarity in your own mind about where interim (and often low-effort) involvement will actually benefit YOU. For example, is there a key proposal you might want to attend? A high-visibility meeting? A key customer interim reach-out? A commitment to people you sponsor to attend the annual performance and bonus meetings?

Which brings me to another point to consider: What's in your yes/no/maybe buckets? For that, let's move on to the next chapter.

Yes, No—and Maybe

This may sound especially detail-oriented, but I really do believe it's worth a little consideration and explicitly writing down your thoughts—(for your eyes only?)—to give you a framework for thinking about planning for your leave. I call it the "hell, no!" vs. "oh, yes!" and everything in between Venn diagram.

Think outside the box. Look for flexibility and options. For example, you may well not *have* to attend that worldwide practice meeting, but it may be in your best (career) interests to do so. And you might actually find the break invigorating, and you can figure out the accounting for it later.

PLANNING FOR LEAVE: YES, NO, MAYBE

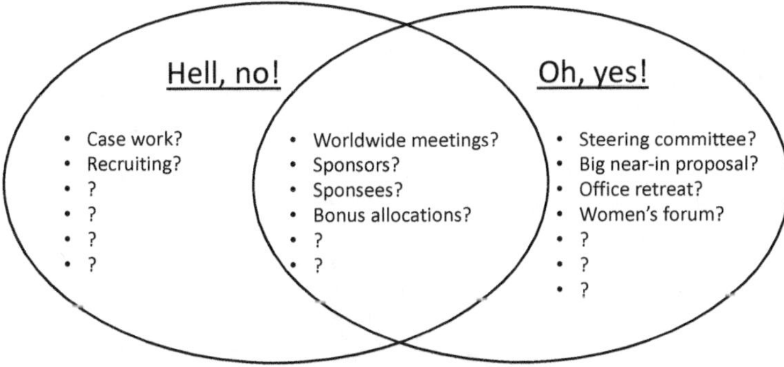

Here's some space for your own diagram:

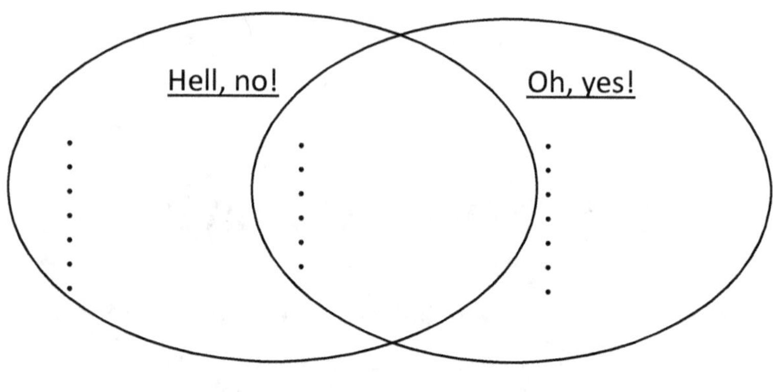

The Handoff

Oh my gosh! I've seen and heard it all. While ambitious, successful senior women executive leaders share so many common characteristics, their approaches to handing off work responsibilities cover the spectrum of possibilities. Perhaps some is driven by the unpredictability of the timing of the arrival, and some is driven by physical, mental, and emotional overload. But it starts well before that—like in months 7 or 8. Here are the stereotypes I have observed:

- **The Ostrich.** The Ostrich carries on with life as usual. She acts as though she is 7 months pregnant (even though she feels like she is 10 months pregnant) and just carries on doing what she is doing. For this type, the possibility of the baby arriving early really doesn't enter her consciousness. She just keeps doing the best she can do today, and she doesn't worry about tomorrow, or next week, or next month. After all, she'll be on leave, and it will become someone else's problem. Right? If you're not intending to return to work, and the exit is anything but graceful (either through your actions or the early arrival of the baby), then being an Ostrich is actually not a bad strategy. But if you are like this, then you may be leaving your colleagues in the lurch. You may be obliging people you don't want to be bothered with in the early days of leave to call/email/Slack you with "just one small but very urgent question" or "just a super quick call to…?" It's kind of a setup for angst—for you as well as your colleagues.

- **The Slave.** Now, the Slave takes a polar-opposite approach. She wants to transition with perfection (think Enneagram Type 3 Achievers) and be of great help to those she leaves behind (think Enneagram Type 2 Helpers). The problem is, not only does she not have to do it all, right up until the end, but she's also probably not actually (ahem…) capable of doing it all. Her body and emotions remind her that she cannot pull all-nighters at this stage in her journey. She enters labor unbelievably sleep deprived and wiped out. And she typically makes her swan-song exit at the most inopportune time. I made mine for my second child with waters breaking at a Senior Leadership Steering Committee meeting, which was, as I now admit, on the eve of my due date. But I kept thinking, *Hey, I got this!* Save yourself the hassle. Admit that there is a ramp-down to entering the likely birth date. Don't try to get everything you possibly can accomplished, with the belief that you will be making it easier on others and helping them out. (Can we say, "a little impending leave guilt"?).

- **The Relay Runner.** Ah, this one I like. She is slow, thoughtful, planned, and realistic. She allows herself to let go, with appropriate forewarning. Her process is smoother, easier, more efficient. However, she can also create a little anxiety as she thinks, *Well, I've handed off a lot of stuff, so now I don't have as much work to do as usual.* Geez, what a problem to have! While your work effort is moving down, your body and emotional needs are ramping up. And that's perfectly fine. Most of your coworkers are, have been, or will be in similar situations;

or at least have extended family who are, have been, or will be. Most of them have empathy and are supportive (let's hope so!). It's perfectly fine not to be too busy in those last weeks. In fact, that may be the best thing to do for your organization and colleagues over the transition phase.

Clearly, I have an opinion about which are the preferrable modes of operation. (At times I have been told that I am not subtle.) Yup, Relay Runner!

Clearly, everyone makes their own choices.

I simply suggest that you become aware of the choices you are making, and the implications for how you will go into your leave!

Just a thought! (As my mother would say when giving clear advice while not wanting to appear that she was. And she was almost always right!)

Photo source: Getty Images/Unsplash.com

Face Reality

We are strong, thriving executive women leaders who tend to have a certain mojo—a passion, focus, drive, direction, love of plans, and adherence to schedules. A need to achieve! And a plan to get there (especially if we happen to be Enneagram Type 3 Achievers). No one can stop us, and if they try, we (sometimes gently, sometimes not so gently) correct them and direct them back into their place.

The great majority of my clients have a "home to-do list." One for all the things to get done before the baby arrives on precisely their due date. (Guess what? They almost never do.) And then one for all of the tasks they are going to accomplish during their leave, from birth-related things like announcements, baby books, and Mommy & Me classes to home-related things like "finish that…"

But the reality is that the vast majority of babies (unless for some freakish reason you totally luck out) will turn out to be (aside from their amazing, love-inducing, cherubic selves):

- Unpredictable

- Unreliable

- Poorly timed

- Sleep sucking

- Demanding

- and Loud!

(I can say these things because you are in that amazing stage of so anticipating the joys of a new baby that you hopefully won't be offended by, or even register, these alternate sentiments and realities.)

Let me suggest you consider revising your to-do list to a "suggestions" list. Now and permanently. The only "do" you are meant to be doing is adjusting to your new life as a mom and providing your baby with the best care you can. So, please, don't drive yourself crazy worrying about accomplishing all the things you might think you can possibly accomplish during this time. At the end of the leave, the world as we know it will not suffer if your suggestions list is still kicking around.

OK, I'll add one caveat to those words of advice: this book. In the quiet (ha-ha!) moments of the day (or at 3 a.m.), consider picking this book up again to think about planning your reentry into work. But it certainly doesn't have to be read now and can wait a month or two.

Last Long Weeks—
to Stop or Not?

I couldn't wrap this short Part Three: Plan Your Leave without commenting on the last couple of weeks of pregnancy. Of course, no one stays pregnant forever, but most women seem to feel like they will be, especially if they are overdue. Two-thirds of all births occur in weeks 38, 39, and 40.

SHARE OF BIRTHS BY WEEK OF GESTATION

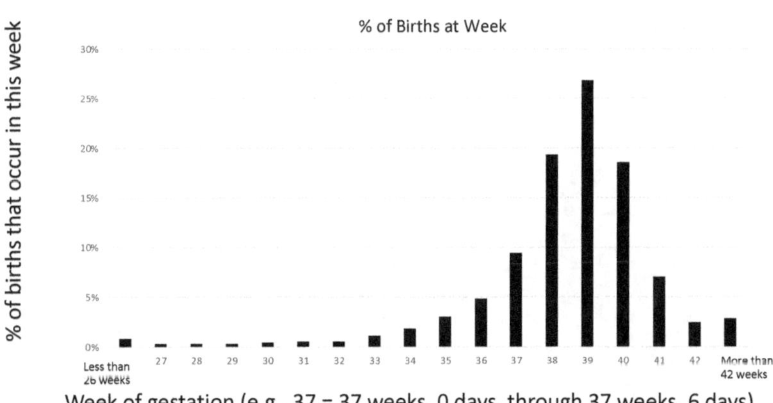

Source: Centers for Disease Control and Prevention

However, even that three-week spread brings in a lot of unpredictability and uncertainty, especially if you tend toward being an Ostrich or a Slave.

In the last month, and especially the last weeks and days, I am way more likely to hear *"How much longer until this happens??!"* than *"I love the glow of pregnancy!"* Though I will also point out that almost none of my clients have fallen into the category of loving being pregnant—and most found the process to be more enjoyable in the context of a means to a wonderful end.

At this point, a statement followed by a question often comes up: *"I am exhausted and tired and fed up. Do you think I should go on leave early?"* Hmmm. Let me start by saying it's not at all about what I think, it's about what *you* think. Or perhaps more important, how *you* feel. You can write down pros and cons about the decision, but at the end of the day, my counsel is to do what feels right for *you* in the moment. When you look back in a year, you probably won't even remember that you took five extra days of (unpaid) leave. In the scheme of your life's journey (and your finances), it really is irrelevant!

So, just do what you feel is best (for you and your baby). Plus, after all, most people are smart enough to know that telling a superpregnant woman that she's wrong about anything is a really dumb-ass move.

PART FOUR

PLAN YOUR REENTRY

Intersection (of You and Them)

At the highest level here, we're searching for and creating the overlap space between *you* (what you want and need) and *them* (what your employer is willing to provide). This is the elusive overlap in the Venn diagram—"The Opportunity" sweet spot. For some, the circles do not meet, yet alone have a significant size for exploration. It's more likely, though, that there is an overlap space—often a large one. We simply need to get honest and creative to find it, and to be brave enough to ask for it. Now is the time to find your Voice.

THE OPPORTUNITY OVERLAP

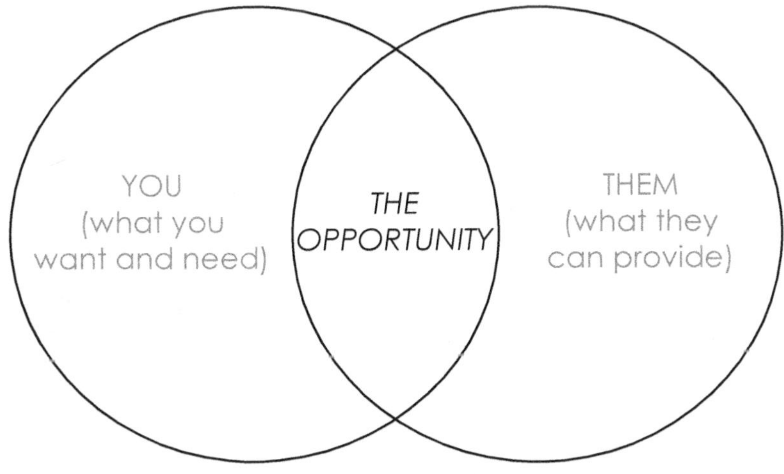

Work/Life Balance Clarity

The term "work/life balance" is heard all over the place and is traditionally used to describe some kind of magical weighting on each side of a scale that gives us a stable, centered, fixed way of steadying ourselves. Delightful and aspirational, right?

Some liken it to a balanced scale.

Photo credit: Elena Mozhvilo

I call BS on this static concept of "balance." It's more like surfing a shape-shifting wave than creating static balance on an unchanging scale.

My observation is that life's journey is not a straight line. It's more like a meandering river, taking twists and turns, sometimes calm and sometimes full of rapids. Sometimes heading straight through the shoot, and sometimes bumping the banks. Sometimes seeking shelter in a quiet tributary.

Likewise for work demands. Sometimes they are intense; other times they are eerily calm. It ebbs and flows. It simply does.

WORK'S EBB & FLOW

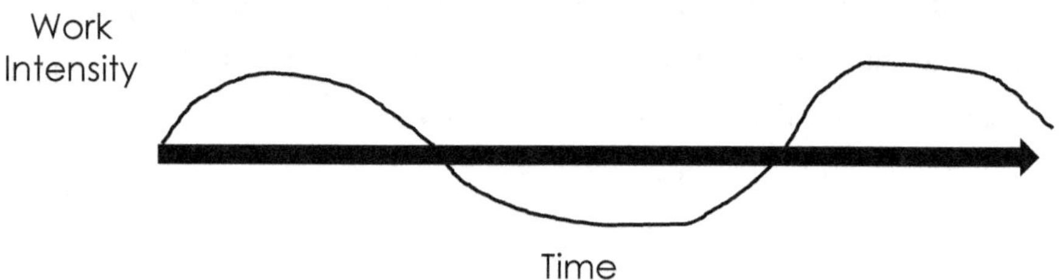

Now, the maddening thing about us high-achieving leaders is that we are incredibly able to create anxiety about *both* phases. Both the ups and the downs. The too busy and the not so busy ebbs and flows. How clever of our Saboteur brains!

- Busy: "*I am so overwhelmed. Work is crazy. I have no time for my family. Everyone is clawing at my time. I have no time for myself. I am exhausted. How am I going to get everything done? No one understands or appreciates me. This sucks!*"

- Not so busy: "*I feel guilty that I'm not doing as much as I should at work. Maybe they don't really need me? What if I get fired? What if someone finds out I snuck out of the office for the afternoon and didn't take a personal day? Maybe I should offer to do that extra project? I'd better look busy, or I might get fired!"*

Pretty incredible when you think about it! So, what to consider about the oscillations:

1. **Accept the phase.** Be aware of what part of the cycle you are in. Know that it will change with time. Decide how long you are willing to stay in it. And decide what (if anything) you are going to do about it.

2. **Reduce the amplitude.** Yes, we all get "busy at work." But how busy is *busy*? Is working all weekend, four weekends in a row acceptable to you? What about one weekend? Or one late night? Know how much you are willing to do. What you, personally, are capable of and what is acceptable to YOU right now.

3. **Manage the length.** Recognize how long it's been going on and set yourself boundaries. You are the boss of you, and at some point (which you decide), you choose to manage yourself out of the phase. Remember, also, that you are likely the culprit in not adhering to the boundaries you set for yourself in the first place. We usually cross our own boundaries before others do (see Chapter 28).

4. **Accept yourself.** Coming back to the stories we tell ourselves in each of the phases, keep those Saboteurs in check. If we're working too hard, we are actually making that choice for ourselves. If we're not working too hard, that lazy sneak-out afternoon is highly unlikely to exceed the many extended evenings and weekends we've put in time in the past. And I've never heard of high-achieving leaders accused of being slackers.

What Will Really Help You Thrive

In this chapter we'll explore:

      A. Outsource What Is Not a Priority

      B. You Get What You Pay For

      C. Work/Life "Balance"—What's Most Important

      D. Negotiables and Nonnegotiables

      E. I Don't Care What You Think of Me

      F. Now Is Not Forever

A. OUTSOURCE WHAT IS NOT A PRIORITY

Many of us (especially those of us with heavy doses of Achiever/ Pleaser/Perfectionist/Stickler/Saboteur tendencies) seem to be under the illusion that we can "do it all." Well, we can't. Especially with the huge added time commitment to your baby. So, forget that *"look at me, I can do everything and do it perfectly and happily"* story to yourself.

The question then becomes *"What can I take off my plate?"* Think back to the earlier chapters looking at your Purpose, what you Value, and your Priorities. Then think about all the things you do—every day, every week, every month, and even every year. I'll bet you'll find a lot of "sand" and "pebbles" in that lower-left corner of your Urgent/Important matrix. You'll likely want to make room for your humongous baby "stone" on the right-hand side. And that is going to require some thoughtful jettisoning.

My guess is that you'll identify things like cleaning the house, mowing the lawn, buying groceries, cooking, etc. If these are things you enjoy, then great, because they must be important to you. If they are not, then outsource them. Seriously. Most of us in senior executive positions have some flex to pay for someone else to do the things that are not meaningful or exciting for us. And the Net Present Value (NPV) is actually quite positive—because it frees you up to focus on the activities where you truly add value and that you get enjoyment from.

If in doubt, try letting go of something for a month. If you truly miss cleaning toilets, then fire the cleaning person and put that back on your plate.

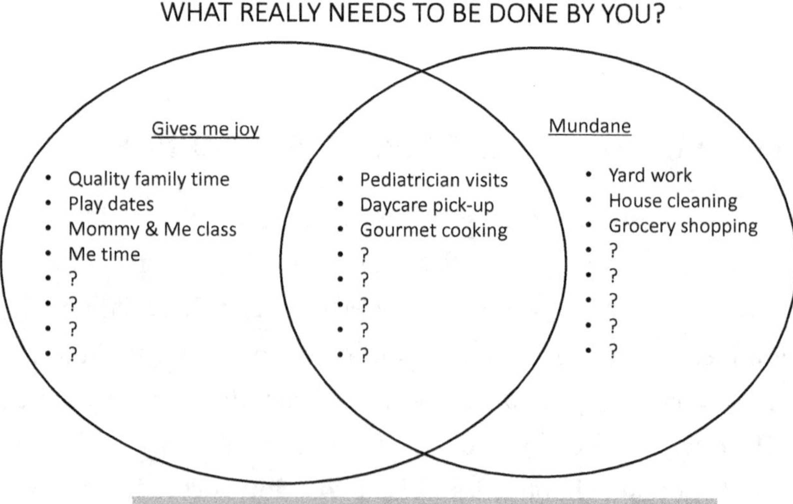

WHAT REALLY NEEDS TO BE DONE BY YOU?

And here's some space for you to jot down your own thoughts.

YOUR "NEED TO DO" LIST

<u>Gives me joy</u>   <u>Mundane</u>

B. YOU GET WHAT YOU PAY FOR

Which gets me to my next point about outsourcing and support. The old saying *"You get what you pay for"* usually holds true.

This topic particularly arises when my clients are speaking about the cost of childcare. Yes, it is an outrageously expensive item. But if you can afford to pay for premium support (which most of my clients can, if they really think about it), then do it. I'm not going to opine on what kind of childcare will best support you and your family. It's such a personal decision, and there are so many options, including daycare, live-in nanny, live-out nanny, babysitter, au pair, at-home spouse, and more.

Let me share the story of one of my clients to illustrate the point about getting what you pay for.

- *Plan A.* About a month before returning to work, "Jenny" and her partner decided that their preferred child-support approach was to hire a live-out nanny. They engaged a nanny-search agency to ensure good screening and broad reach. They offered market rate ($20/hour) and created a job description with the help of the agency, really thinking through what was most important to them and their new bundle of joy. All went well for the first month. Until suddenly, it didn't. Their nanny informed them on a Friday evening that she was quitting, effective immediately. Although she had enjoyed working with them, she had found a position that provided more pay, fewer chores, and more predictable hours. Jenny and her husband were dumbfounded and in shock. Then the reality and the anxiety set in. It was panic time.

- *The Transition.* Scrambling over the weekend, they found no suitable candidate. They were stuck. Jenny had a flight out for an important client workshop on Monday. Luckily, her husband, "Ben," had a little more flex, with some available days off that he had to use. His employer was not happy about his suddenly taking time off, but it was doable. By Wednesday, the agency had been able to find some temporary resources, but each new person, in each new week, meant re-explaining the job (and reestablishing trust).

Both Jenny and Ben were stressed. So stressed. And if they were truly honest with themselves, they were both pretty distracted by work. And feeling guilty about the quality of care for their baby, and the quality of their work outside the home. It seemed that they were thinking about their daughter every hour and hoping that she was OK. Texting, stressing, agonizing. So: Roll in Mom. Moms are amazing and often step into the chaos at a moment's notice (mine sure did, repeatedly, as did my aunts and best-friend-cousin), especially for their precious first granddaughter/second cousin. But moms have lives, too—and not everyone wants their mother-in-law living with them forever (even the best of them!). They all felt stressed, even though Jenny and Ben's daughter seemed none the worse for it.

- *Plan B.* Jenny and Ben, at their wits end, decided to up the pay to see if they might attract a more qualified group of candidates. They (gasp!) went from $20 to $30 an hour. It may sound outrageous. At a $10 difference, for 40 hours a week, that was $400 a week. $20k a year. Crazy on the surface. But when Jenny and Ben (who made $300k a year between them) looked at the finances, it was less than 10 percent of their joint income. And guess what? Over a dozen candidates applied in the first 24 hours. They interviewed half of them, and would have been happy to hire three of them. The one they selected turned out to be amazingly qualified (experience, character, alignment with their philosophies), and to be very loyal and predictable (higher-paying alternatives did not present themselves and tempt her to leave). They also set more realistic expectations about the need for flexibility and that the role would not always be 9 to 5. So far, "Amanda" has been with them for nearly a year. The relationship provides the stability they want for their daughter, the reassurance that their nanny will not be leaving on short notice, and the ability to deliver in their careers with excellence. In fact, the bonuses they received at year's end (for performance they believe they were only able to achieve with the stellar support of Amanda) more than offset the premium price they chose to pay. Not to mention how quality of care and peace of mind play into it.

I'm not going to presumptuously tell you what to pay your nanny. I just ask you to consider the true cost-benefit of hiring the quality support that works best for you and your family. Sometimes, we can be quick to jump the gun with *"Oh, we can't afford that!"* But can you afford not to?

C. WORK/LIFE "BALANCE"– WHAT'S MOST IMPORTANT

Before considering the kind of support you need, and the kind of work situation you will put yourself in, it helps to get crystal clear on the key stress factors that work contributes to your life. To simplify it, there are three primary drivers:

- *Sustainability.* How many hours you will work, over what period of time. The volume of work over the year (and the remaining hours in a week you will have to do other things).

- *Flexibility.* The extent to which family needs and desires can be dovetailed into traditional work hours. The seamlessness of integrating life activities into the workday (and vice versa).

- *Predictability.* How often work emergencies crop up and plans change at the last minute. The ability to anticipate the demands of work and to plan the week's schedule well in advance.

How important is each of these to you today? Prioritize the list by understanding why each matters to you. Consider the circumstances of any partner in the equation, and how that might shift what you need for yourself and for both your careers at this point in time.

Thoughts to self:

____

____

In addition to flexibility, sustainability, and predictability, there are other intangibles that might be critical to your satisfaction with your career role. For example: inspiration (excitement, engagement, challenge) or affiliation (friends, inspirational leaders, social outlets). Pause for a moment and think about what those might be for you. Why is it that you want to continue your career in the first place? And yes, you can add "money" if that's one of the motivators (or even the primary one!) driving you.

WHAT MATTERS MOST RIGHT NOW AND SOON?

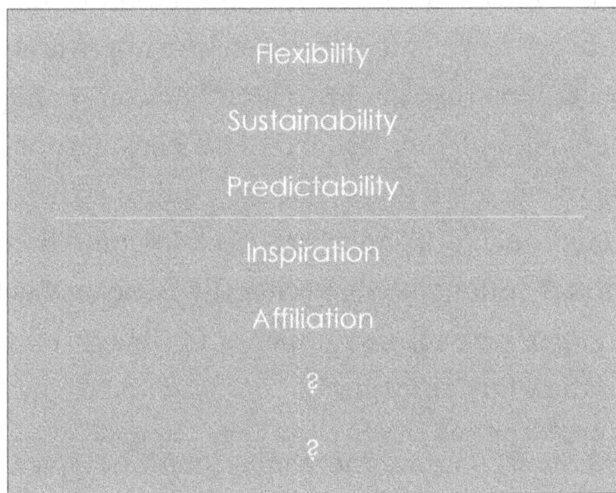

Notes to yourself about what matters most to you in your desire to return to work:

All these underlying needs and desires (sustainability, flexibility, predictability, other) are typically translated into policies and expectations along five dimensions. Understand what these are for your employer and think about their implications for the underlying "what will really help me thrive" factors you just explored. Here are the five (sometimes unwritten) expectations to look for and consider:

1. *Workload:* The standard workload is typically about 2,000 hours per year (40 hours a week, 50 weeks a year). But what's is the "typical" week? Is the expectation in reality more like 60 hours/week? Is it 6 days/week? Understand the workload expectations (usually unwritten but commonly held beliefs/experiences of your cohort). Also consider that, a 50% part-time role in a job that typically requires 80 hours a week may be a reasonable 40-hour-per-week job (and the premium pay for the premium job that is usually associated with long hours but super-high all-in compensation may well be great compensation for "part time"!).

2. *Work hours:* Some companies publish typical work hours (e.g., *"9–5 with a 30-minute lunch break"*). Most also have culturally typical work hours (e.g., *"we're usually in the office by 8, but done by 6, with a couple of hours on the weekend"*). Know whether there are certain expectations, particularly with global companies across multiple time zones (for example, super-early mornings for West Coasters working with

Europeans, super-late nights for East Coasters working with Australians). Be aware of any expectations about Saturdays (Middle Eastern affiliates) and Sunday evenings (Asia Pacific affiliates). They are what they are, and be aware of what the cultural expectations actually are. You are highly unlikely to single-handedly shift the company's cultural norms.

3. *Regular PTO:* This can range from two meager weeks to more than six weeks (with tenure, especially in European countries). Know the policy, but also know the (sometimes unwritten) caveats that come with it. Know whether you can "buy" extra vacation, or take a sabbatical (paid or unpaid). Some companies encourage taking large time blocks (for example, insisting that at least one time block be a minimum of two weeks); others suggest taking only shorter time blocks (for example, with a midweek check-in, or an expectation to sift email daily). Some expect you to shut down the laptop and be entirely gone; others expect at least some availability for those "critical calls" (are they really?). The point here is to understand the actual culture behind the written PTO policies. And to think about how that expectation fits with what you know best rejuvenates you and gives you joy. And whether you will choose to consider going counterculture (someone has to be the first).

4. *Physical location:* While many companies now have a WFA (work from anywhere) approach, even more have strange matrix policies like *"be in the office at least three days a week"* or *"everyone must be in the office on Wednesdays."* There are all kinds of (often not ideal) practices out there. And they seem to migrate and change with experimentation (and as justification for those long, large office leases). Know what your company expects, and how that impacts your life and your choice

of living location). It's likely not realistic (for you or for them) to be the only employee who *"doesn't do Wednesdays."*

5. *Travel:* This one is rarely written into job descriptions, and even less commonly written into a corporate policy. But the expectation is real and can vary widely by role and by client case assignment. So, it's a bit murkier, but tends to be more situation-specific and therefore more negotiable in setting expectations. Please don't avoid having the conversation about travel, even if it can feel a bit awkward. Think about what you can tolerate (or might even look forward to!). For example:

- The annual retreat that takes you halfway around the globe for 10 days (and do you really need to be there live)?

- The out-Sunday-back-Thursday on-the-ground-at-the-client commitment (and can you be assigned to another type of client, at least in the short term)?

- The two-days-every-other-week scenario? Is that two days, with one overnight in between? Or two very long day trips, but you're back at home in your bed?

The permutations (and possibilities) are endless. So, know what you want and ask for what you need at this point in your career.

D. NEGOTIABLES & NONNEGOTIABLES

Let's get a little more tactical about these priorities, needs, and wants. What does it mean for your discussions about returning to work?

A useful exercise is to consider what "I MUST have" (nonnegotiables) and what "I'd LIKE to have" (negotiables). Get crystal clear on it. Write it down on the template below. Come back to it. Ponder it. Really establish in your own mind what these are.

Take into consideration that these are not "forever and a lifetime" decisions. These are what are important to you in your reentry—say, for the next three to six months. Priorities change and you can always revise the list. Note that this "time frame" context will be important in your planning for reentry discussions, covered later.

Here's a laundry list of the factors some of my clients have considered:

- NO travel

- Never working past 6 p.m.

- Not being available 5–7 p.m.

- Not working weekends

- Going to Mommy & Me on Thursday afternoons

- Not taking calls after 11 p.m.

- Working from home when my child is sick or the nanny no-shows

- Not attending weekend company retreats

- Accommodating planned childcare activities (e.g., doctor' appointments)

- No in-person meetings (unvaccinated COVID concerns)

- Not attending evening recruiting and social events

- Working from home three days per week

KNOWING WHAT REALLY MATTERS TO YOU!

NEGOTIABLE	**NONNEGOTIABLE**
•	•
•	•
•	•
•	•
•	•
•	•

E. I DON'T CARE WHAT YOU THINK OF ME

This one was a touchy topic for me for quite a while (and it took me a while to even realize it). As an Enneagram Type 3 Achiever, I was always pushing myself to be the best, the fastest, the most spectacular. I had way overachieved academically (skipping three grades of school, graduating from college as one of three female Genetic Engineering majors at age 20, earning a Harvard MBA with Distinction), and then in my career (coveted Procter & Gamble Brand Manager, then Boston Consulting Group consulting career, culminating in becoming Managing Director & Partner, fast-tracked, and transferred between four offices, Lead Officer for the global Organization and Consumer Practice areas). Not to brag, but to share the track record and expectations I had set for myself.

And so it was that I found myself walking through the cafeteria of BCG's Chicago office, having recently been promoted to Manager in the New York office, and getting ready to kick off a major global acquisition piece of work for a top consumer packaged goods client. On a roll and feeling awesome! Having taken two maternity leaves (three months and seven months) and having worked in various part-time and full-time capacities over the previous three years, I was feeling comfortable in my fast-track trajectory. Although "behind-time" in elapsed years and months (and a full cycle behind my peer cohort), I was actually "fast-tracking" it from a full-time equivalent of months of tenure.

Then I heard them—huddled together at a table in the cafeteria: the team that was to become my new hot-shot A-team to tackle this challenging case. The scene went something like this: *"Well, I heard she may not be very good because she's really behind on promotion track. She's been here for over five years, and she only just made Manager. I hope we're not in for incompetence here. Those people are a nightmare to work with."* I just about imploded. Well, I didn't, but I did go to the restroom and have a good cry. A really good one. The injustice! The unfairness! My ego was crushed with the knowledge that others thought I wasn't a superstar.

I got over that one (the case went well). But I still got that jealous sinking of the stomach as I watched my peer group get elevated to the next level up—and then even two levels up from where I appeared to be stagnated. It was irritating. Then downright annoying when someone who had worked for me a couple of years back was suddenly my boss. Huh? Wow, reality check. Ego blow!

At some point, though, I had an epiphany and changed my perspective. I knew the truth. My career development and promotion advisors knew the truth. And in most ways, it didn't matter what other people thought about my career track. In fact, most people don't even think about my career track, except perhaps in passing.

When I really stopped and thought about it, I was on the amazingly fast track of life. My life. I had made choices that made the most sense for me, and I was loving my life. Others who had made different parent-path choices and continued flat-out in their careers may have looked like superstars. But they were often saddened by the role they were able to play in raising their children and being a real part of their family.

So, if you plan to work anything less than full time, be prepared to put your career progress in the context of your life context—what your Purpose, Values, and Priorities lead you to know what you want and choose to do.

Oh, and don't forget to put your ego in check!

F. NOW IS NOT FOREVER

Unlike diamonds, maternity leave and return-to-work plans are not forever. They are not hard, cold, set-in-stone plans to last a lifetime. They are malleable, they change. Life happens. Shit happens. If you get yourself all caught up in the next decade's plan, there will be so many unknown variables and surprises that you'll have a hard time planning it all out with perfection. It can become so confusing and overwhelming and unmanageable.

Give yourself a break. What will work for you and your family today? For now. Maybe the next three or six months. Yes, we need to consider the impact of the decisions we make today on our longer-term life and career goals. But we may spend too much time fretting about the "what-ifs" and not enough time thinking "just for now."

It's helpful to couch the conversation about return-to-work in the context of the first few or several months. Some of the nonnegotiables we may have while our children are infants and babies are temporary. And it's easier for an employer to say yes, for example, to "no travel," if there's a time frame on it and we're not asking for a commitment forever.

You Are Not Alone

In this chapter we'll explore:

A. WORK RESOURCES

There are many resources to help leaders lead within an organization.

All types provide valuable input; however, each role is explicitly different, and it should be clear in your own mind. The four primary roles are highlighted below.

WORK SUPPORT RESOURCES

Sponsor	Advisor
A person who is <u>responsible</u> for, and <u>investing personal capital in</u> the actions, development, and career path of another. • Internal • Ongoing promotion • Vested support in success • Mutually beneficial to highlight the "good"	*A person who helps another decide on or plan a course of <u>action</u> for a <u>particular topic</u> of their expertise.* • Internal or external • Discrete soundbites • Incentives can be mutually intertwined • Personal opinion, "good or bad"
Mentor	**Coach**
A person who gives another advice on <u>actions</u> AND has the personal relevant expertise to tailor <u>career</u> advice. • Internal or external • Ongoing relationship • Incentives can be mutually intertwined • Full transparency (the "good" and the "bad")	*A person who dovetails their broad external perspective, with deep personal understanding, to guide another's <u>actions in life AND career path</u> choices.* • External • Holistic, integral "work" and "life" • Deeply personal relationship • Full transparency (the "good" and the "bad")

First, make a list of who performs each of yours roles. Seriously, write them down.

Sponsors: ____

Advisors: ____

Mentors: ____

Coaches: ____

Peers: ____

Others: ____

Now think about what communications you have had with them recently. When did you last check in and say hello? Are you still top-of-mind with them?

- How can they help you?

- What can they share about anything that's shifted in your absence?

- Do they have any words of wisdom or advice for you?

- What might you be able to offer to support or help them?

- Have you set up time to reconnect (live or virtually)? And what will your agenda be?

Think of it like a key stakeholder management plan. Communication is key. And people, at least nice people, are happy to help but won't do so unless they know how to be helpful and you've set up time with them.

Key actions you will take, and by when:

____

____

____

____

B. LIFE RESOURCES

There is so much wisdom, knowledge, and experience around us to support us working-outside-the-home moms. Not to mention the mistakes made and lessons learned from those who have journeyed the path before us. It's not like we're the first one to navigate this. Yet we can sometimes get all caught up in our independence and a false belief that we can solve every problem ourselves. Why would anyone want to reinvent the wheel? Or spend time learning a skill that we are highly unlikely to ever use again (toilet cleaning, anyone?). There are experts out there for that.

Here's are some examples of the types of *external resources* that are out there to support return-to-work moms. It is by no means exhaustive—and I have no personal incentive to endorse any of the brands mentioned. It's simply that they are loved by more than one of my clients. What's on your list?

RESOURCES FOR SUPPORT

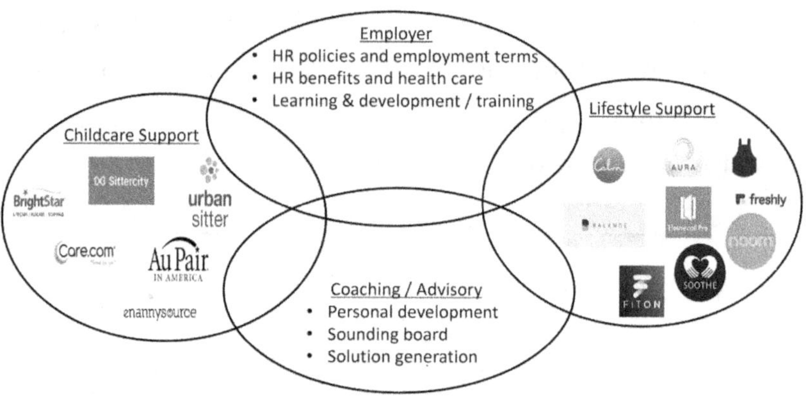

Take a moment to jot down what support resources you think might be helpful to you. Make a list; decide how/when/what to do to leverage them. Don't be shy. As the saying goes, "*It takes a village.*"

In addition, and often way more significantly and importantly, *friends and family* can provide support. Many of them have been through this return-to-work journey before us and they can provide a wealth of support—both in terms of advice and experiences and in terms of just being there for you (and letting you grab a nap!). I was lucky enough to have both my mum and my cousin in residence for most of those early infant (sleep-depriving) days. In most cases, grandmas are highly enthusiastic volunteers who are more than willing to help out you, your partner, and your baby. Don't underestimate their helpfulness and value! Use them wisely, and clearly communicate what you need (and where your boundaries are).

C. READING RECOMMENDATIONS

Along the client-journey I've heard recommendations for favorite pregnancy and parenting books. I have no vested interest in any of them (and people look at me oddly when I read them in public, since I am clearly not of an expecting age anymore).

Here's a list of pregnancy and early-parenting books my clients applaud as must-reads:

- *Expecting Better: Why the Conventional Pregnancy Wisdom Is Wrong—and What You Really Need to Know* by Emily Oster. Fantastic statistics, facts, and myth-busting!

- *Moms on Call* by Laura Hunter. Great book on schedules (and the logic behind them). A three-part series (0–6 months; 6–15 months; and 15 months to 4 years) of great wisdom on creating predictability (can anyone say "sleep schedules"?).

- *1000 Questions about Your Pregnancy: Everything Every Expecting Woman Needs to Know* by Dr. Jeffrey Thurston. Straightforward, humorous, and informative.

- *What to Expect When You're Expecting* by Heidi Murkoff. An oldie but updated classic. Even I read this during my first pregnancy (ahem…) 25+ years ago. At least it's not from the "Dr. Spock" era. (Ask your grandma about that if you haven't heard about him.)

- *What to Expect the First Year*—you guessed it, also by Heidi Murkoff!

D. DOUBLE SAFETY NETS

I'd like to highlight something here: Life is unpredictable, but babies are even more so. And the margin for error is a bit slimmer with newborns. The anxiety and guilt for "getting it wrong" can also be bigger and much more significant for you and for the baby.

I encourage you to think through the "what if?" scenarios, because if all kinds of things *can* happen, then the chances are pretty good that a few of them *will* happen. It's a fine line—I certainly don't want to encourage you to be a doomsday-imagining Chicken Little running around with your head cut off. But a little preparation forethought can go a long way. Here are some examples:

- If your nanny suddenly falls ill or quits, what are you going to do? Is the first call to your friend or to your mom? Is there a backup plan, or is the plan *you* (or your partner)?

- If your little one were to get sick next week, who is going to stay home with them? Consider sharing calendars and flex for who's on point for any contingency plan—well before it surprisingly happens.

- If you think you'd like to have date night every Friday, have you got a permanent standing order for a sitter? (Which you can always cancel with enough warning, or pay for the option to have the unused availability.)

- If one caretaker starts at, say, noon, and the other ends at, say, noon: Does it make sense to build in a 15-minute overlap? It may be better to have double coverage than no coverage.

You get the idea. Not to make anxious, scenario-planning worriers out of all of us. But my learning over the years is that if something *can* happen, it most likely *will* happen—you just don't know what and when. So, a little forethought goes a long way to preventing scrambling, disappointment, or disasters.

E. SOMEONE STARTED THIS IN THE FIRST PLACE

Speaking of the "others" in your life, many of you will have partners (or baby daddies) to take into consideration. You've probably been doing a lot of "me" thinking alone (unless your partner for some reason is reading this book with you), and you may in fact have another critical "other" to consider (and to leverage). All this cool thinking does not have to be done alone. After all, this baby was not created alone.

Throughout the exploration in this book, we have focused on "I" (you!). Who you are, your current employment situation, your leave, and your reentry. All this thinking is, of course, grounded in thoughts about the imminent arrival.

If you do have an involved partner, their opinion counts too. Consider sharing with them the "ahas" you may have surfaced during your exploration here. Consider asking them if they would like to take some of the assessments (such as the Enneagram) and explore some of their wants and desires. Understand what their point of view might be. Life for them too is about to take a dramatic shift.

If you are truly in a partnership, each of your actions will impact theirs (remember the canoe analogy back in Chapter 4?). Most partners are heavily involved in raising children, and often will have their own angst and concerns about taking their Parental Leave (or whatever it is called at their place of employment). They too might be interested in reading this book.

Not only will each of you be going through major life transitions, but your relationship will be too. While I am not a licensed marriage therapist or relationship expert, what I do observe is that it is all about communication, communication, communication—with a good dose of clarity and patience. And it never starts too early. Consider vulnerably sharing your thoughts and trepidations about your journey.

Here are some examples of what my Parental Pivot male clients have commented on:

- *"I was happy (but nervous) to have my leave."*

- *"Some people think paternity leave is like some kind of free vacation, and I feel like they looked down on me for taking it."*

- *"This is lovely, but insane."*

- *"My wife has become a little crazy."*

- *"The baby is uncontrollable."* (Really?!)

- *"I can't pull all-nighters anymore."*

- *"We have zero time to ourselves now."*

- *"I love it, but it's crazy!"*

- *"I never thought we'd both be so sleep deprived."*

Remember: Partners Are People Too! What's your partner thinking and how are they doing?

Exploring Options

In this chapter we'll explore:

        A. Laying It Out

        B. Inference Ladders

A. LAYING IT OUT

Hopefully by now you have spent quite some time considering all the possibilities. And hopefully your head is not spinning, and you haven't worked yourself into a state of extreme anxiety. Let me start by reminding you that nothing (nothing!) is fixed, irreversible, or unchangeable. You're just looking for the options that best suit you (and your partner) and your baby. It's a stake in the ground for now, not a lifetime commitment.

If you're sure you know what you want and it will work (for now), carry on and get cracking.

But if you're sure you know what you want and it's just not going to work with your current employer, then resign. Without guilt. And start polishing off that résumé in search of a place where you can be you, and you can make the choices you want to make. It's your life to live, and we don't want to make choices that we already know are going to make us miserable.

If, however, you are now rather confused about what the heck to do, lay it all out—on paper. Think of the possibilities and distill them down to two or three options. Then think about the pros and cons of each. It may sound rather simplistic, but simplification can often add clarity. Here's a template and some space for thinking it through. Use a pencil and an eraser—it will shift and evolve as you ponder it.

OPTIONS!

1	2	3
Pros + + + + + Cons - - - Unknowns (things to figure out) * * *	Pros + + + + + Cons - - - Unknowns (things to figure out) * * *	Pros + + + + + Cons - - - Unknowns (things to figure out) * * *

B. INFERENCE LADDERS

At this point, I believe it's worth taking a brief, self-imposed time-out (It will be great practice for when you are dealing with "time-outs" for a toddler.)

While exploring options, we can sometimes get inside our own heads and make assumptions about our "others" (employers, partners, other support resources).

You may have heard this before: We are experts at creating our own "inference ladders." Meaning that we make assumptions about how others think and feel, and therefore about what they are or are not willing to do. We set the narrative in our own minds and then expertly look for confirming points of evidence, often connecting the dots in a somewhat pathological way. From this, we weave our warped view of reality and thus limit the art of the possible.

So, if you hear yourself thinking thoughts like *Oh, they will never consider that*, or *This would never work*, reconsider. Are you making assumptions about what is and is not possible, in a world where opportunity might abound with good exploration, consideration, and communication?

My suggestion here is to pause and consider whether you are climbing any inference ladders. And if so, how to step back and consider how the narratives of others might differ from yours.

Photo credit: Tommy Bond, Unsplash.com

The Ask:
Engaging in the Conversation

In this chapter we'll explore:

     A. Position of Power

     B. Power Pose

     C. Finding Your Voice

     D. "No" Is a Complete Sentence

     E. A Gentle Warning on Timing

A. POSITION OF POWER

Surprisingly to me, many women seem unaware of their *position of power*—or even worse, fear that they might be asking for special treatment or favors around accommodating their need for modified roles as they enter this important parenting phase of life and parental adjustment. Nothing could be further from the truth! Let's start by looking at the downside of becoming a mom, from a career perspective.

- *The Downside: Maternal Bias.* We ALL hold biases (derived from stereotypes, which are actually quite helpful from an evolutionary perspective). I could write a whole book on biases, their origins, their applications, and their downsides, but I'll leave that for another day. Biases are subtle but real and are often referred to as "micro-biases." They exist, they are meaningful, they are prolific, and they are typically unconscious. Of particular note for expecting women is "maternal bias," which is the tendency to find mothers and pregnant women less *competent* and less *committed* to their jobs. It's out there, be aware of it, and challenge it if you see it.

Source: Shutterstock.com

- *The Upside: Over-Indexed Interest.* The even weightier factor for women, though, is the strong desire to retain high performing/high potential women ("HiPos"). In general, and all else being equal, most companies have an interest in retaining women, particularly more senior women, and especially women of dual minority status (race, country of origin, sexual orientation, etc.). Broadly, the reasons behind it include:

- Women continue to be underrepresented, particularly those with seniority.

- DEI (diversity, equity, and inclusion) is high priority for most organizations.

- Companies have invested a lot in your development.

- Regrettable loss is expensive.

- Formal and informal flexibility continues to grow.

Therefore, young lady, please do NOT go into your discussions or negotiations apologetically and looking for a handout. Go in confidently, with head held high, knowing that it's as much in the company's interest to find a way to retain you as it is in yours to find a way to thrive at work.

B. POWER POSE

Ah, the Power Pose. This is pretty much the sister to, but the opposite of, the Grounding practice: getting yourself calm, present, and settled, which I mentioned in Chapter 1.

It's scientifically demonstrated that the state of our body impacts the state of our mind. So, if you want to show up with power and be fully present for a meeting, it makes sense to prime your body to feel strong.

This nifty exercise takes just one minute. The science shows that it must be done for at least 60 seconds (which really isn't that long). And it really can be done anywhere. I've even done it in the bathroom stall before a live meeting. Um, yes, really.

The idea is to take up as much physical space as we possibly can for at least one minute, while gifting ourselves with delicious, empowering thoughts. Note that this "*take up space*" thing is not something we women often do, and that our presence can already be diminished by our typically smaller bodies than those of our male counterparts.

So here it is: Stand with your feet placed wider than your hips. Reach your arms up and out, spreading them as high and wide as you possibly can toward the sky. Tip your head back a little and look upward. Take a deep, deep breath in and expand your chest forward. Feel this physical power and think strong thoughts such as "*I am strong,*" "*I rock,*" "*I have this,*" "*I am a superstar.*" Have fun with it; laugh a little. Even shout it out loud, depending on where you are! Keep it up for at least 60 seconds. Then stand back down and notice how you feel. Powerful. Strong. Ready to seize the moment. Pretty amazing stuff for one minute!

Photo credit: Ryan Moreno, Unsplash.com

C. FINDING YOUR VOICE

Some of us will come into a reentry conversation confident, clear, and full of resolve. But not always. Others may feel a bit anxious or nervous about what the outcome of the conversation might be. For those of you falling in the latter camp, let me remind you that you've been through a process of discovery to know what it is that you need to live in that opportunity space at the center of the Venn diagram of "You and Them" (Chapter 22). You are clear in your own mind what your options are, and what is and is not negotiable.

So many good books go into depth about having great conversations. Here's a distillation of my favorite suggestions and reminders to consider in any conversation.

- *Be honest:* Speak and act the truth.

- *Be direct:* Speak in terms that are clear, concise, and focused.

- *Be present:* About the here and now.

- *Be personal:* Share about you and yours.

- *Be sincere:* With heartfelt compassion.

- *Be a great listener:* Attentively, respectfully, and without interruption.

- *Be real:* Acknowledge what you don't know or understand.

- *Be candid:* Forthcoming about uncomfortable things.

- *Be consistent:* Always.

- *Create opportunities* for dialogue.

- *Don't be judgmental* (especially of yourself).

Given all your thoughtful consideration and a clear ask, chances are your employers will say yes or navigate to a modified yes solution that works for both of you.

But let's say they say no. Don't panic. That's OK. If it wasn't going to be the right fit for you, then it wasn't going to work out in the longer run. And it's better to find that out now, without putting yourself through weeks, months, or even years of trying to put that proverbial square peg into a round hole. You are a strong leader, and many other organizations out there envision roles that will work for you. Shift to Plan B—finding the right place to work!

D. "NO" IS A COMPLETE SENTENCE

No.

There, see? Short, succinct, to the point. Try it again, this time with a little expressiveness. You can even practice saying it out loud in the mirror.

No!

Many of us have a hard time grasping this concept. Especially women, who tend to be more community oriented. And particularly Enneagram Type 2 Helpers (whose identity is tightly wrapped up in helping others and saying yes too much).

So, for those of you who have a hard time with the "no" thing, let me introduce you to a slightly softer concept: The Power of a Positive No.

A simple "no" can at times leave us feeling a bit uneasy or harsh. Here's another way to think about saying no without simply and directly just saying no. The Power of a Positive No is essentially a "yes-no-yes" sandwich.

1. *YES:* Find and state the common ground. The "yes, I hear you/such a request has some logic or common goal" acknowledgment. Do not just generically state, "yes, and…" Instead, specifically identify the "agreement" piece that you are acknowledging.

2. *NO:* State clearly that you will not accommodate the entire request. Clearly. No waffling. And not necessarily with an explanation for why (unless you feel it's appropriate).

3. *YES:* Offer an alternate solution, idea, or suggestion that might help the person out with their request. (And one that is aligned with your values, and often doesn't have to involve you!)

Voilà! Here are a couple of (abbreviated) examples:

- "I understand the importance of getting the analysis done ('yes'). However, I cannot work on it this weekend ('no'). I can get it to you Monday by 10 a.m.—would that work? ('yes')"

- "What a great idea to play outside ('yes'). No, you may not play on the street where there are cars speeding by ('no'). Why don't you play in the backyard? ('yes')"

If you struggle with saying no, consider practicing this whenever you don't want to use "No" as a complete sentence, or you're tempted to just say yes because it's easier. You'll find that with time and practice, it begins to flow more naturally, and it will save you a lot of time by not doing the things you don't have to or want to do.

E. A GENTLE WARNING ON TIMING

Maybe I should have put this warning right at the start of the book:

"It's never too late to get started!"

"The early bird catches the worm."

Some of you may have picked up this book and thoroughly read and digested it before entering your third trimester (more likely so if you are an Enneagram Type 3 Achiever!).

Some of you may be doing all the work as the question arises or feelings shift during your leave. That's good too.

But then there are those who have procrastinated. Remember the Avoider Saboteur? Yup, that's what might be going on there. It manifests as one of two camps:

1. "I don't want to think about it yet/I'm busy on my leave/I'll get to it and make a decision the week before leave is over."

2. "Well, I'll just say yes to whatever they expect, and figure it out when I'm back"

Both are dangerous. If you don't explore what you want, don't find a voice to ask for it, and don't actually maintain your boundaries, it usually turns ugly fast. So, don't subject yourself to it. Get your head out of the sand and make this a priority. It's never too early to start, and at times the discussions can become multiple and iterative. Give yourself the gift of time.

PART FIVE

THE TRUTHS ABOUT RAMPING BACK UP

Boundaries:
Your Own Worst Enemy

Photo credit: Robert Linder, Unsplash.com

Whose boundary is it, anyway? It's yours. Employers have far less incentive to hold the boundary than you do. After all, it's your life!

We all set boundaries (implicitly or explicitly) with work, with children, with partners, and with a lot of others.

Work boundaries often come down to the three underlying drivers of work/life balance that were highlighted in Chapter 24. Recall:

- *Sustainability*: how many hours, on average, we will designate for "work."

- *Predictability*: how often work plans change, and with what kind of warning.

- *Flexibility*: how much traditional "work hours" can flex to accommodate non-work-related needs.

Most of us, either explicitly or intuitively, are weighing and drawing those lines with our employers. Employers recently have often become much more receptive to accommodating requests if we have the courage to find our voice and ask for what will work for us.

Setting boundaries with employers (both hard, like a concrete wall, and soft, like a strand of yellow warning tape) is often the easy part.

The tricky part is setting and maintaining boundaries with ourselves. Yup, the person sitting right here with us. We define boundaries, get buy-in from our work teams. And then choose to run into or step over them ourselves.

- Sometimes it's *fear* of repercussions (like promotion-track timing).

- Sometimes it's just spontaneous *excitement* in the moment (like a super-engaging problem to finish analyzing at midnight).

- Sometimes it's just *neglect* (it creeps up, we ignore it, and somehow, some day, we lift our heads up and realize we've drifted from our own intent).

So, the big question is: What are you doing to keep *yourself* in check?!

Successful People Fear Failure

Photo credit: Michael Mouritz, Unsplash.com

We've all heard the term "fear of failure." But have you ever really thought about it for yourself?

What makes successful people successful is that, well, they've been successful. Top of Class, A-Performer, risen to the top, accelerated progression, a Superstar, a High Performance/High Potential Rising Star. All good stuff.

But what many hyper-successful people have not contemplated is that they are often not good at failure. They have pretty limited experience with it. They don't know how to handle the setbacks that other mere mortals may have experienced often (!) during their rise to midlevel management.

How many of our top leaders typically encounter career trials and tribulations—and *failure* (gasp)? How many of us failed and failed and failed again, and then rose to the top? Not many. It's not that some amazing examples aren't out there, but, as a whole, our top leaders have limited experience with the big F-word: Failure.

High performers sometimes discover that they can be quite risk averse—that they actually fear failure. They don't put themselves in positions where failure is a real outcome. They would rather steer the ship slow and steady than place a big bet or take a chance. They would rather not try a new activity or hobby that they're not experienced with or good at, because they might not look perfect in their attempts to learn. Someone might laugh at them. So they miss out on a lot of growth and a lot of fun.

You're about to enter into a whole new territory—parenting. And there will be failures and missteps and bumps along the road. Both in your work and in your life. And that's OK! It's hard to imagine real growth without any failure. If you never fail, you're probably not really pushing your growth-edge.

What's your fear-of-failure factor? What have you tried recently that you're not likely to succeed at, and might even look silly doing? It's OK to fail. In fact, it can be liberating.

Hopefully, you will have some (not too traumatic) failures. Because if you don't, you're unlikely to truly be exploring life along your journey.

What would you do if you knew you could not fail?
—Robert H. Schuller

Excellence Is Not Perfection

Photo credit: Matthew Schwartz, Unsplash.com

"Excellence is the result of caring more than others think is wise, risking more than others think is safe, dreaming more than others think is practical, and expecting more than others think is possible."

A poster of a soaring eagle, with that inspirational inscription by Ronnie Oldham, has hung on my office wall for decades.

Striving for excellence is so very aspirational and keeps us on our growth-edge. However, the quest for excellence does not imply the quest for perfection. We hyper-achiever types often push ourselves to do it all. To make it perfect. To answer everything. We of course want to keep moving forward with agility and speed. However, the cost of getting the last 10% perfect, or even more the cost of getting the last 1% perfect, can be very high. It can sap our energy away from other activities and indulgences that delight us.

So, next time you are pushing yourself for Excellence, take a moment to pause and ask yourself whether you are actually pushing for unnecessary (and costly) perfection.

Emotional Regulation

Big transitions like becoming a new parent are not for the faint of heart. It can be an emotional roller coaster of feelings. Expect it, roll with it, talk about it, and take time out for you.

The most common not-so-nice feelings my clients share at points during their reentry are anxious, overwhelmed, insecure, discouraged, and even angry. OK, so that makes it sound like returning to work will be awful overall. It won't be.

Clients share that they have deep appreciation, for the most part, for the important role that outside-the-home work plays in their lives. Most delight in and love the contribution that their careers provide to their holistic selves. It's part of who they are and how they grow.

But there will be some not-so-good days and even more not-so-good moments. Just as there were before parenthood—but these times are driven by different events, they can be more of a surprise, and they can be amplified. As my parents often said, "This too shall pass." Here are some suggestions for when those not-so-nice feelings arise:

SUGGESTIONS FOR REGULATING EMOTIONS

Anxious	Focus on the present moment and take deep breaths. Search for root causes and reality.
Overwhelmed	Write down what needs to get done, based on importance & urgency. Focus on one task at a time.
Insecure	Focus on appreciating and accepting yourself, flaws and all. Give yourself credit for who you really are and quell the Saboteurs.
Discouraged	Be kind to yourself. Remind yourself of the reason why you are trying.
Angry	Pause so you can give yourself space to think clearly. Respond rationally instead of reacting and going up inference ladders.

Stop, pause, ground
Question FEAR (Future Events Appearing Real)

Sustaining It

By now, hopefully, you have been through all the exploration and preparation and should be well on your path to a successful reentry into the world of work and career.

Let me leave you with a final reminder. Life evolves, journeys migrate, things change, and shit happens.

Just as you would take stock of your career through annual performance reviews, so might you review your life journey and progress. So, as you reenter the workforce as a new mom, may I suggest that you put a note to self on the calendar to stop, evaluate, and adjust how life is moving along.

Truly, we are each the "CEO of me," and it's worth pausing to reflect on it. Just do it now. Get it on the calendar for a month or two out: "*A meeting with me.*"

Photo credit: Manasvita S, Unsplash.com

Ready for Round 2?

OK, I just couldn't resist it—having "Round 2" as a title. Just kidding. I am sure, as you approach that feeling of "*will this pregnancy last forever?*" or "*will my baby ever sleep through the night?*" the last thing you want to think about right now is the possibility of doing this again.

But I will just point out that as you contemplate what works best for you and this imminent or recent arrival, it's worth considering what the longer-term path might bring. For some, this is "*one and done.*" For others it's "*wait and see.*" For most, it's "*who knows?*"

So, not to put the cart way ahead of the horse, there is always the opportunity to consider these ponderings in the context of the bigger picture of what you anticipate and hope will possibly happen next along your journey.

Just saying it.

Please don't feel like hitting me.

Words of Wisdom

I asked my Maternity Magic and Parental Pivot coaching clients to share a sentence or two about their most critical insight in managing the transition to motherhood as it related to working in fast-paced environments.

Here's what they had to say:

- *"Many of us are achievement-oriented, which makes it hard to 'just be,' but try not to put too much pressure on yourself to accomplish a lot of personal stuff during your parental leave. If the only thing you're able to do is spend quality time with your new baby during this time, that's amazing!"*

- *"Pumping and working is harder than being pregnant and working. Seriously consider how the decision to stop (breastfeeding) coincides with the decision to start (working)."*

- *"I think the biggest thing I learned (other than how to power nap) was how to try not to be a perfectionist."*

- *"I was actually kind of surprised that they (the company) agreed to everything I asked for. And so far, so good. It's really working for us."*

- *"I was well aware of the emotional/hormonal impact of being pregnant (like the hormonal changes of becoming a teen), but I was unaware of how my hormones would change, and my feelings would just sort of put themselves out there when I first returned to work. It's OK to cry. Just go find that 'wellness room.'"*

- *"I thought I'd be tired, but that's an understatement. I was exhausted. And so was my husband. Being new parents was not always the nirvana we thought it would be. But it's so worth it!"*

- *"Work used to be my everything. Now it's just one thing. And it's not to say that my dedication to work shrank. Rather that the pie grew, and I now have a more balanced set of priorities and a much richer life."*

- *"I learned the importance of taking time for myself. For just me. Rather than spending every last minute with (my daughter) to soak in those last moments, I am glad I took a week to get myself together before going back to work."*

- *"I didn't realize I was actually, fundamentally, a control freak. Until my totally uncontrollable, unpredictable son came along. Don't even plan on getting out the door on time anymore. Or at least build in an extra 30 minutes that you never seemed to need before."*

- *"I was pretty good at carving out 'me' time, but not so good at carving out 'us' (husband) time. Sometimes we just have to stop and cuddle and remember why we wanted this in the first place."*

- *"Don't let moms (or mothers-in-law) stay too (too) long!!!"*

PARTING THOUGHTS

PARTING THOUGHTS

Enjoy being, not doing
Take it easy
Forget perfect
Pursue what works for you
Find your voice to ask for what works for you
Make it work … for now
Share your experiences and wisdom with the women
who follow

Have fun and enjoy the now!

If I can be of further service to you, please do reach out!

With love and support for you on your journey,

Anna

Key Topic References

TOPIC	PAGE

TOPIC	PAGE

Key Topic References　★　228

About the Author

Anna Minto is an executive advisor focused on empowering executive women to thrive in fast-paced environments. She is the founder of Transformational Change, as well as You Are Possible, which provide coaching and executive advisory services, motivational workshops, and inspirational speaking. Her clients include executives from Fortune 500 companies and professional services firms.

She has an MBA with distinction from The Harvard Graduate School of Business, is recognized by the International Coaching Federation as a Professional Certified Coach, Integral Coach, and Enneagram Coach, and is a train-the-trainer of Infinite Possibilities. She spent 17 years with The Boston Consulting Group, including time as Managing Director and Partner.

Find out more about You Are Possible at YouArePossible.club

— *Contact* —
ANNA MINTO
Executive Advisor & Collaborator,
Founder of Transformational Change & You Are Possible
aminto@TrChange.com • (214) 263-0234
linkedin.com/in/annaminto • YouArePossible.club
TrChange.com

Please reach out to me if I can be of service to you

www.ingramcontent.com/pod-product-compliance
Lightning Source LLC
Chambersburg PA
CBHW071502140726
47997CB00005B/1824